Shatterproof

SHATTERPROOF

7 POWERFUL PRINCIPLES TO RISE ABOVE ANY STRESS & CRISIS

CONRAD DRAPEAU

Copyright © 2017 Conrad Drapeau
All Rights Reserved

ISBN 13: 978-0-9976749-0-3 (trade)
ISBN 13: 978-0-9976749-1-0 (ebook)

Published by Horizon Press.
8837 Zurigo Ln.
Naples, FL 34114 USA

All trademarks and registered trademarks are the property of their respective owners.

Cover design by CB Messer
Page design and layout by Chinook Design, Inc.

10 9 8 7 6 5 4 3 2 1

*This book is dedicated to the person who inspired
me to get my message out and had the most
impact on me, Carol Drapeau (1952–2009)*

CONTENTS

Acknowledgments

To all of you who put yourself out there in sharing your stories: Annie, Elizabeth, April and Bob, Linda and Mike, Francine, Rob, Chris, Mel, Brigitte, Armel, Randi, Marie-Lou, Matt, Madeleine, Paige, Len, Andrea, Chrissy, Lima, Bob, Oldrich, and Dale. Some names have been altered by request. (I hope I didn't miss anyone.) Without your powerful stories, *Shatterproof* would not exist. Thank you!

To Ilse, who has dedicated her life to serve others, who taught me so much about the body and mind, and who has been instrumental in giving me practical tools that have served me throughout my life. Thank you!

To Chris, who has been a big supporter and contributor from the beginning of my writing journey—and our work and friendship will continue for years to come. Thank you!

AJ, it's been a long journey together but we finally got this done. Your editing skills and sequencing of the stories has made *Shatterproof* the quality read I was seeking from the beginning. Your ability to help me get my message out for maximum impact is most appreciated. Thank you!

A special thanks to my daughter Carie, who has been a huge part of my life, who has endured so much and yet has always maintained a sense of humor and dignity. You are truly an inspirational example for all of us to follow and admire. And thank you to my grandson Ethan, who is the most loving and hardworking person I know. You touch me and bring a smile to my heart each and every day.

And to someone special to share this precious life with—Liz.

"What we call the beginning is often the end.
And to make an end is to make a beginning.
The end is where we start from."

T. S. Eliot

Introduction

What would you do if you suddenly lost eighty percent of everything you had worked for? I remember the call as if it happened yesterday. "Conrad, the files are gone, your money is *gone*." As I listened to our financial advisor's panic-stricken voice, my mind racing a mile a minute, I tried to focus. I asked for details, but there was no comfort in his response, no explanation that made any sense. By the time I hung up the phone, I was in full-on crisis mode.

In what seemed like the blink of an eye, we were almost completely wiped out. We had lost *millions*. The people we entrusted with our investments had betrayed us, and life would never be the same. Isn't this the way crisis hits us—in the blink of an eye? Whether because of a relationship challenge, a health issue or financial or work stress, your world can turn upside down in seconds. Even when we know that change is coming, it almost always at least *feels* sudden.

As is true for anyone who experiences loss, hardship or difficult circumstances, my wife Carol and I were left reeling with the news that most of our hard-earned money had disappeared seemingly overnight. I was in a state of shock, frantically trying to piece together what happened while figuring out how to keep our house and pay our basic bills— things I hadn't worried about for some time.

Getting the call that nearly all of our money was gone could have broken me.

But it didn't.

Shortly after the initial shock and several sleepless nights, I was able to recover from this crisis, adjust our life to the "new normal," and regain the peace and happiness I enjoyed before we received our devastating news. It wasn't because I am just "one of those people" who bounces back. It was because I already had the emotional, mental and spiritual resources to deal with crises.

In response to previous crises, I had developed a simple but powerful "Shatterproof System" to navigate, manage and rise above any crisis. To support that system, I also incorporated mental and physical exercises to help shift my thinking, mindset and perception. Practicing and applying these skills in my daily life gave me a strong foundation, and my Shatterproof System gave me the tools to handle anything— so that when Carol and I were faced with losing almost all of our money, I was able to approach the event with perspective and confidence, feeling in control.

Within a short period of time, our entire "space" changed. We sold our home, my wife began taking self-help classes and I was presented with an exciting new job opportunity. Even though the battle with our former accountants and money managers continued, we had gained control of our lives. We were shaken, but not broken. We had entered what I came to call the "Shatterproof Zone."

The Shatterproof Zone is a place of impenetrable calm, where you can be free from stress, chaos and noise and cultivate a quiet confidence that enables you to stay fully present and experience joy, love and happiness, no matter your circumstances. In this space, you can deal with almost any crisis, stress or challenge.

In today's society, more and more people are prisoners of their minds, living in a very different space, a stress-fueled zone. The consequences of crisis-induced stress are expansive; that stress affects nearly every aspect of our lives. When you're stressed out, your energy is depleted. This causes low productivity, poor cognitive function and emotional distress and, if sustained over time, can contribute to the development of serious health conditions including chronic or fatal illnesses. Stress kills joy, contentment and overall well-being and often leads to depression, anxiety disorders and other more severe mental illnesses.

Simply put, if you can't handle the crises that come your way, they can wreak havoc on your life.

At the core of crisis-induced stress is a sense of being overwhelmed, of feeling out of control, which leads to insecurity and a lack of confidence. Suddenly, life just seems harder to navigate. You're less likely to make positive choices, move your life forward, take action to solve problems or do what it takes to make your life *better*. It's like walking through life as a shadow of your former self, fearful of all that *could* happen.

When you are living in this stress-fueled zone, with your sense of self and capability diminished, one more crisis could break you.

We are not taught how to cope with crises in school, yet all of us will face a major life crisis at one time or another. The purpose of this book is to make you aware of the crises and stresses in your life, and then introduce you to an effective system that will not only help you cope with your daily challenges, but help you come out the other side of the crisis stronger, wiser, happier and better equipped to handle whatever comes your way. In essence, this book will help you become *Shatterproof*.

I was never more grateful for my Shatterproof Zone than when, just a few years after we lost the money, Carol and I received more life-altering news.

"You can't leave the hospital," the nurse said. "We tried calling your doctor and we can't reach him. You need to go to the emergency room. The doctor there will explain the results of your MRI and what type of immediate action is required."

Carol had been experiencing headaches, but nothing could have prepared us for the devastating news that we were about to receive. I was never more grateful for the tools and resources that helped me enter and stay in the Shatterproof Zone than I was at that moment and in the months to come.

You already possess all that you need to be able to become Shatterproof; you have simply not yet tapped into the Shatterproof Zone. Accessing this space is not complicated; it's not a state reserved for special people, or devout people, or well-educated people or lucky people. By following the system outlined in this book, anyone can become Shatterproof, even—*especially*—you.

You and only you can get to the Shatterproof Zone. I am simply a messenger providing guidance. Whether you opt to sit back and let crises take you down or tune in and take action, it's your choice. I hope that today, or tomorrow or at some point as you read through the stories, practices and strategies outlined in this book, you will make the choice to take action.

I know you will get there, because you've already taken that first step by reading this page in this book, right here and now! I've intentionally written this book to be an easy read that enables you to shift your mindset, take action quickly and see immediate results. So all you have to do is get going!

Once you begin on this path, you instantly become aware— and that awareness will guide you as long as you continue to participate and practice. The awareness then becomes part of you and, without even realizing you've changed, you'll be living the Shatterproof life. When you work on yourself and learn to know and tap into the source of strength within you, living a Shatterproof life will become completely natural to you.

The stories you are about to read were selected to support the key messages in this book, the Seven Coping Principles you are about to learn. These stories cover many common crises and challenges—stress-fueled anxiety attacks, job loss, loss of fortune, loss of a spouse, loss of physical ability, loss of a parent, loss of a child, divorce, infidelity, drug addiction, rape and still more. The brave individuals who allowed me to interview them want to serve you in the same way I do—

to provide you with the ability to connect, reflect and gain a different perspective on how you can handle stressful situations. You may never have to endure crises like those described in this book, but you will undoubtedly experience stressful events. My hope is that these stories will inspire you and motivate you to move forward and take the right steps toward becoming Shatterproof.

Shatterproof is simply a formula, a GPS to direct you toward a new way to look at life. It is a new approach that will enable you to deal with any minor or major stress and most types of crisis and challenge, whether you have experienced them in the past, are experiencing them now or will have to face them in the future. The tools offered to you in this book are simple, impactful and sustainable.

It's taken me five years to write this book and more than twenty-five years of practice, study and research to *prepare* to write this book. I've read and researched thousands of studies, scientific papers, journals, articles and books covering the mind and the brain; stress, disease and sickness; psychology, cognitive behavior, physical and mental health; human behavior, communication and relationships; and various world cultures and work cultures.

Throughout my twenty-five-year career connecting people with technology, I've studied human behavior among thousands of people throughout North America, the United Kingdom and Asia. I've had many successes and gained wisdom and knowledge through my many challenges and failures. These have included being demoted and being fired; losing a ton of money and, as a salesperson, being rejected thousands of times; becoming the primary caregiver for my terminally ill wife; and coaching my daughter through the challenges of raising a special needs child after divorce. I've traveled to Japan, China, Korea, Thailand and India, fed the poor, and studied these countries' cultures and ancient teachings. And I have worked on myself for more than two decades with the guidance of a master teacher.

It took me twenty-five years to learn how to quickly bounce back from any stressful situation. Fortunately, you won't need to put in that much time. This book is the essence of everything I've learned, the easy, actionable principles and practices I have culled from research and experience that will help you become Shatterproof.

Over the last five years, writing *Shatterproof*, I created well over a thousand pages of content, way too much for people to digest in a single book. What you're reading is the distillation of my message, the simplest version of the tools I offer, condensed so that the Seven Coping Principles can be easily digested and adopted in your everyday life. When put into practice, these principles will transform you bit by bit, in a sustainable way.

I am not a psychologist, or a doctor or a spiritual leader. I am simply a man who, out of necessity, developed a simple system to ensure that no matter what happened, I would be able to cope and not break. Beyond that, the system enables me to shift my thinking during difficult moments so I'm able to maximize the personal growth I gain from every event. Now I'm sharing this Shatterproof system with you so that you can do the same—so that you can not only stay strong in a crisis situation, but grow from every challenging experience you have. I'm sharing these tools so you can gain the courage, confidence and control to face any stressful situation, knowing you'll be able to manage it and get through it quickly.

I hope you'll take the next step, and then another and another, so that you too can become Shatterproof.

BEFORE WE BEGIN...

What does it feel like to be Shatterproof?

Imagine yourself able to access a state of calm and mental focus at a moment's notice, allowing you to think clearly and draw your focus to the things that need attention. No matter how difficult the situation, you are able to face it with confidence. You are able to release any tension, restlessness and anxiety related to stressful events.

Imagine being able to diffuse and counterbalance any negative emotion—anger, frustration, envy, fear, worry, anxiety, mistrust, sadness, depression—before it takes hold and has a chance to harm you and affect your life and overall well-being. See yourself able to release any resentment you may feel toward others before hatred and anger set in. You have the ability to experience more patience, kindness, openness, trust, love, joy and happiness at a moment's notice, almost as if by your command.

Imagine having the courage to make tough decisions and choices whenever required. You can tap into your creative powers instantly and approach any stressful situation with acceptance and resolve. You are able to perform your day-to-day activities and duties with renewed energy, vitality and contentment.

Imagine spending less and less time thinking of the negative past or worrying about the uncertain future. See yourself moving on from rejection and failure easily, and without lasting negative impact. You feel empowered, which gives you hope and confidence to overcome difficulty and accomplish whatever you need, wish or want. You accept and adapt to change and disruptions with ease.

This is a mere snapshot of what it feels like to be Shatterproof, and the process to get there is simple, powerful and proven. Are you ready to begin?

Chapter 1

What Most People Don't Realize About Crisis

One Tuesday morning, after a lovely long weekend with my wife, I arrived at work early to get a head start on the week ahead. The frantic pace of working at a technology start-up meant twelve-hour days for most of us, so my four-day weekend seemed like a mini-vacation. As I sat down to listen to my voicemails, I felt relaxed for the first time in over a year—until I heard the first message.

"Conrad, Prudential is kicking us out! You told me last week that everything was under control," my boss screamed into the phone. "I just spent the last two days trying to figure out what's going on and couldn't reach you. From here on out, I'm taking over the account. I don't want you talking to them anymore. When you get in, call me immediately!"

I was totally shocked; I was sure that we were on track with Prudential and that everything was going well. My stomach turned into a massive knot, my heart raced and my mouth felt as if it was lined with cotton. As I walked to the bathroom, I could hear the voicemail message repeating in my head. I was all clammy and sweaty and when I reached the bathroom I splashed water on my face and looked up at my reflection in the mirror. "What just happened?"

We've all faced moments like these. Our reactions to unpleasant and unexpected events take us down a negative path, an emotional roller coaster ride that is often painful. Staying on this ride can lead to a downward spiral. In this state, we lose our ability to think clearly, our decision-making capabilities diminish and our confidence quickly erodes, leaving us feeling insecure, anxious and convinced the situation is out of our control.

Would most people categorize this episode as a crisis? Probably not. And yet my body didn't know the difference. You might be surprised to learn that your body generally reacts to stress the same way, no matter how severe your mind perceives that stress to be. According to the HelpGuide. org article "Stress Symptoms, Signs, and Causes"[1] by Jeanne Segal, PhD., an online resource in collaboration with Harvard Medical School, "The body doesn't distinguish between physical and psychological threats. When you're stressed over a busy schedule, an argument with a friend, a traffic jam, or a mountain of bills, your body reacts just as strongly as if you were facing a life-or-death situation."

Fortunately, at the time this incident occurred, I was already practiced at entering the Shatterproof Zone, so I was able to get off the roller coaster ride well before I lost my grip or the confidence to believe that I could manage the situation and create a positive outcome. My disciplined mind was able to enter the Shatterproof Zone almost immediately and focus on how to get through the crisis as quickly and painlessly as possible.

DEFINING CRISIS

"Crisis" is a word that has been given a serious beating by modern society. If stress is something we are afraid to admit to, then crisis is the modern equivalent of leprosy. Even those of us who think they may be in crisis are often afraid to admit it to colleagues and loved ones.

Assigning the word "crisis" to a stressful situation may seem unnecessary, and it's certainly scary. We associate the word with emergency rooms and the six o'clock news and we think, "*Those* people are in crisis, not me."

We also fear the consequences of admitting we're in crisis, as if the moment we admit it to ourselves and others, nice men in white jackets will come and take us away to a padded room. We believe that crises are for people who have lost their capacity to cope. We think, "I'm functioning just fine, thank you. No way I'm in crisis."

So what is crisis, anyway? Here is the definition of crisis, according to Dictionary.com:

1. A stage in a sequence of events at which the trend of all future events, especially for better or worse, is determined; turning point.
2. A condition of instability or danger, as in social, economic, political, or international affairs, leading to a decisive change.
3. A dramatic emotional or circumstantial upheaval in a person's life.

See that? No mention of mental breakdown or men in white coats.

Most of us associate crisis with the third definition—drama and upheaval. We think of car accidents, disease, job loss, natural disasters, divorce and the like. But let's look at the first definition. "The trend of all future events" refers to what will happen next, but it's the unknown that is the root of all the stress in our lives. Any time we're unsure of an outcome, we're experiencing some form of crisis. We experience this on a regular—sometimes daily—basis. Will I land the big client? What if he doesn't call me for a second date? What if I fail my test? How will my kids react to the news that we're moving? What if the check *isn't* in the mail?

It may seem silly to characterize these "everyday" moments as crises, but I can tell you that when my boss accused me of dropping the ball with our biggest prospect, it sure seemed like a crisis to me. My body reacted to the stress of the unknown. What if I can't get the prospect back? What if I lose my job? What if I can't get another job? How will I support my family?

While I was chatting with my friend Annie, she told me she had just witnessed a car accident in front of her house: A school bus had stopped short, which caused the car behind it to slam into the back of the bus. She was shocked that the bus actually left the scene and immediately ran out of the house to see if the other driver was okay.

"She wasn't hurt, but she was a mess. After we called the authorities, she explained that this was a rental car she had been driving because her other car was in the shop for repairs after another accident," Annie explained. "I couldn't calm her down—she was crying and caught up in 'what ifs.' 'What is my husband going to say? He's going to kill me. What is my insurance company going to say? They'll probably drop me! I'm never driving again!' There was nothing I could do to make her realize it was not the end of the world."

As I listened to Annie recount more of the story, I thought about how it's not the event or circumstance itself that is most stressful; it's fixating on the myriad ways in which our lives could change as a result that causes the most stress and upheaval. The accident was over and the driver was fine, yet

In certainty, there is no crisis.

her mind was racing, conjuring up every possible consequence. Experienced this way, a crisis brings on a deluge of negative, often irrational, thoughts. On and on they go, until your heart rate is up, and you can feel a headache starting just between your eyes. And, after the adrenalin wears off, you are likely to feel overwhelmed and tired, which may lead you to be hard on yourself and short with others.

Annie finished the story, sharing what the police officer said in response to the driver's frantic worry. "He looked at her calmly and said, 'You're going to be okay. That's why they call them accidents.' I thought of you, Conrad, and how this woman certainly would have benefited from being able to access her Shatterproof Zone!"

The police officer was calm because he deals with car accidents every day. He knows all of the potential outcomes and he knows that, unless someone has been seriously injured, it really *is* going to be okay. He doesn't have a feeling of uncertainty, because his experience has filled in all of the blanks. Most crises are unfamiliar to us, so we have no idea what to expect; even an angry phone call from a boss or a fender bender can be a classified as a crisis.

Let me be clear: Defining crisis in this way does not diminish the experiences of those who would most certainly define crisis as a dramatic upheaval. Dramatic upheavals happen every day, too. But again, it is the not knowing what will happen *as a result* of the upheaval that has the most impact on our lives.

Think about the last time you got so caught up in the "what ifs" that you felt stressed, or scared or experienced physical pain or discomfort like nausea or a headache. Now, what if you had actually known the "trend of future events?"

What if you knew with absolute certainty why your boss called you into her office, or what your child's teacher would say at the next conference, or whether you got the promotion, or how many more months your home renovation would take? Would you have the same reaction? No, you most definitely would not.

In certainty, there is no crisis. And in the Shatterproof Zone, you can be sure of two things: You will feel confident that you will be okay, no matter the outcome, and you will have far more control over the situation and your reactions than you ever thought possible.

FOR BETTER OR WORSE

The second part of the first definition—"the trend of all future events, especially for better or worse, is determined"—is also something we usually don't associate with crisis, at least not when we're in the thick of it. But it means that, although the result of the crisis could make things worse, it could also make things better! So, in effect, the very *definition* of crisis indicates that perhaps the event itself could ultimately result in a *better outcome*.

Crises almost always put things in perspective. After the initial shock wears off and the immediate requirements of the situation are handled, most people experience, at least on some level, a feeling of gratitude for the many blessings in their lives. This is certainly life made better by crisis, if only for a moment.

You may also experience tangible outcomes after a crisis that make life "better" for you in some way. Your new job may be better than the one you lost, for example, or a health scare might bring about a healing in family relationships. We can't know the outcome of a situation, but there is a chance that a crisis will ultimately lead you to say, "It was a blessing."

Of course, we don't run through possible positive outcomes when we're stressing about the unknown; we just worry about all of the negative potential scenarios. Like the woman in the minor fender bender, we allow negative thoughts to run unchecked, and those thoughts lead to stress—stress the body reacts to in the same way it would react if that fender bender were a tragic car accident.

Realizing that the outcome *could* lead to something better, even if we can't conceive of what that might be at the time, allows us to change the negative thoughts in a conscious way, and in turn, change our reaction to the crisis.

TURNING POINT

The last intriguing component of this definition is its end: "turning point." Most of us have a positive association with turning points—we think of them as the moments when things change for the better. If, as discussed earlier, we acknowledge that a crisis could lead to something better—an affirmation of love, a renewed sense of faith, the discovery of an aptitude or strength you didn't know you had or even something more tangible or measurable—we can see how the ultimate "something better" is experiencing the crisis as a turning point that leads to a positive change.

How many stories have you read or watched on television that feature characters who were suddenly inspired to improve their lives in some way because they experienced tragedy?

> *Crises almost always put*
> *things in perspective.*

Crisis often inspires us to take action, to follow dreams long dormant, to make a difference in the world, to get healthy, to heal relationships, to make amends, to start over in a meaningful way. In this way, crisis can be the turning point that not only changes your life for the better, but helps you become who you were always meant to be.

Even on a small scale, a turning point brought on by crisis can have an impact on your life. We all know that even the best-laid plans require adaptation. As we work hard toward our goals, we hit roadblocks (crises) that force us to tweak our plans. Turning points, by their very nature, are opportunities to make changes—some big, some small—that will help us continue on our paths toward our goals and purposes.

In fact, it is difficult to picture a turning point *without* a crisis. When we're winning the football game by twenty-five points, we keep doing what we're doing. It is only when the tables turn, and the threat of loss is imminent, that we look for alternative solutions—alternative solutions that could, in the end, be just the strategies to help us win the game.

It has been said that the only true path to breakthrough is breakdown. Crisis, experienced as a turning point, pushes us out of our comfort zones (often against our wills), forcing us to evaluate and take action. Like baby birds pushed out of the nest, we are forced to fly.

COMING OUT OF CRISIS

In the moments after I received the message from my boss about the potential loss of a major account, my mind raced with possible negative outcomes, and my body was in shock. Yet once I acknowledged I was in crisis, I immediately went into my Shatterproof Zone. Drawing on the process I had developed over years of study and practice, I splashed water on my face, took a few deep abdominal breaths and ran through the Seven Coping Principles. While drying my face, I said aloud:

"I don't know or understand why this is happening, but I do accept that this is a necessary experience for me to live through. I am willing to learn and be open to whatever knowledge and wisdom this experience will teach me that is absolutely essential for my growth, evolution and life purpose. As difficult as this situation may be, I will embrace it and make the best of it knowing there's a higher purpose—despite the limitations in what I'm able to see or understand at this stage."

When I returned to my desk a few minutes later, I immediately began applying the Principles. By the end of the day, I had uncovered the source of the problem (a misunderstanding brought about by a poorly written email) and resolved the situation, and our largest prospect was still firmly on track to work with our company.

Not all problems or crises disappear this easily or quickly, but your reaction to the problem or crises *can* be managed easily and quickly when you follow the Coping Principles and learn to enter your own Shatterproof Zone. And, though some situations are out of your control, you may discover that you are able to create a positive outcome *because* you are in this state. Using the Principles enabled me to break free from the

> *I was able to stay in control despite the chaos and panic around me.*

negative thought patterns that could have consumed me and to direct my attention in productive and useful ways. I was able to stay in control despite the chaos and panic around me. Even if I had been unable to resolve the situation, even if we'd lost our largest prospect, I would have been okay. That is what it means to be Shatterproof.

1. Think back to a recent stressful experience. How did it affect you physically? Mentally?

2. How did you react to the event?

3. What was the outcome of the situation: better, worse or no change?

4. How did your reaction have an impact on that outcome?

Note: I created a free workbook for you, so that you can answer these and other questions and track your progress in one place. You'll also find helpful exercises. To download your free copy of *The Shatterproof Workbook*, go to shatterproofbook.com/resources.

Chapter 2

Five Common Traps of Crisis

At age thirty-five, after a fifteen-year career in human resources, my friend Linda decided to make a major career move and buy a local interior decorating business when it went up for sale. Her first day in her brand-new store was a shock; she'd always had a passion for decorating, but had no professional experience in design or retail.

"Here I am, sitting in a brand-new store with eight hours of training. I would look out the window, waiting for clients to come in," Linda told me. "Looking around the empty store, I started thinking, 'Oh my God, what have I done? I gave up a good corporate salary, pension and benefits to do this.' The reality of the situation brought me to tears."

Linda pushed on for the next nine months, but her anxiety only got worse. She gave in to her fear of the unknown and let the stress of handling everything on her own get worse. "I wasn't eating or sleeping well; I lost twenty-five pounds. Then one night, I snapped, and my husband had to take me to the emergency room. I lost it. I had a massive anxiety attack. That's when they put me on antidepressants."

Whether you've experienced a major crisis or multiple mini-crises spread out over time, it's easy to let the effects of crisis alter the quality of your life. It's easy because you have the perfect excuse to allow this to happen—after all, you're in crisis!

While the effects of crisis and the feelings you have about the situation seem perfectly justified, hanging on to them for any length of time may be a trap from which it could be difficult to break free. Linda had fallen into two of the common

What the mind thinks, the body believes.

traps of crisis: *stress* and *loss of control,* and getting stuck in those traps began to take a toll on her, mentally and physically. Her thoughts and feelings about her career and financial crisis landed her in the emergency room.

There is a saying: "What the mind thinks, the body believes." While it's perfectly understandable that you might feel any number of the emotions discussed in this chapter, getting stuck in these "traps" will eventually take a toll on your mind—and consequently, your body. Fortunately, there is a simple, effective way to get out of these traps quickly or avoid them all together. But before I share the Seven Coping Principles with you, I'd like to point out five common traps that you can easily fall into, so you can be aware of them.

STRESS

According to WebMD Medical Reference "The Effects of Stress on Your Body,"[2] up to ninety percent of doctor's visits are stress-related. Stress is best described as the body's reaction to a change that requires a physical, mental or emotional adjustment or response. It can come from any situation or thought that conjures up negative emotions, including, for example, frustration, anger, nervousness and anxiety.

In Western culture, stress is often tagged with a negative connotation. We view stress as a sign of weakness or a problem that we need to "deal" with. Drug companies have manufactured powerful medications to help people try to cope with the effects of long-term stress, and a visit to any bookstore will reveal shelf after shelf of books and self-help guides designed to help in one way or another. It is, however, far too often overlooked that stress is not the cause of the problem; stress is a symptom of something else.

If you've ever broken a bone, you know the pain is excruciating. What if, rather than go to the emergency room to treat the break, you decided to pop a few pain pills and just deal with the pain? That would be ridiculous, right? You'd have to deal with the problem, or the pain would remain, and your bones would likely never heal correctly, right?

Stress is a symptom of an event that somehow caused what you are feeling. There are those who will want to argue this, but when you start to dissect the symptoms, you will see that you can track every one of them back to an *event*. These events are not necessarily major, life-altering moments; in fact, most of the time they are not. Most of the stress we feel on a daily basis is just the outcome of the culmination of many small, passing events. A snide comment made by a coworker, a negative comment from a loved one, a deadline that got pushed up, something you put effort into that didn't bear fruit, expectations not being met, a lost file on your computer, someone cutting you off while driving—nearly anything can be a contributor to our feelings of being "stressed."

Stress, your body's reaction to crisis, is meant to be helpful. It gives you the energy and clarity to face your fears—which can help you with everything from asking someone out on a date to saving your own life when threatened with danger. Yet any level of stress has negative consequences when sustained, as explained in Sue Shellenbarger's article in *The Wall Street Journal*, "When Stress is Good for You":[3] "[Stress] can propel you into 'the zone,' spurring peak performance and well-being. Too much of it, though, strains your heart, robs you of memory and mental clarity and raises your risk of chronic disease. A little stress is helpful for peak performance, but too much can literally shut down the brain."

It's understandable that you would feel stressed when faced with a crisis, and it's also completely normal to feel that stress in your body—an upset stomach, a sleepless night, a racing heart—as you deal with shock or fear of the unknown. However, to avoid the negative impact of stress on your mind and body, you'll have to let go of stressful feelings before you get stuck. Facing the challenge of operating a business she knew little about caused Linda tremendous, prolonged stress, so much so that her mind—and her body—reacted dramatically. She got stuck in a common trap of crisis, and her mind and body paid the price.

LOSS OF CONTROL

Perhaps the greatest contributor to prolonged stress is the feeling that we have no control over the outcome of a crisis. Feeling out of control, as if your well-being is dependent on the whims of others, is a terrible and terrifying feeling. It's as if you're a hostage to the situation. Giving in to this "out of control" feeling impedes your ability to cope, to focus and to make decisions. Eventually, panic sets in, and the crisis begins to take a toll on your body, mind and spirit.

In this state, no amount of good advice or comfort will help. Friends and loved ones may urge you to "relax" or "trust that everything will work out," but their well-intentioned words are usually the last thing you want to hear. You think, "Relax? You want me to be calm right now? Are you kidding

> *In this state, no amount of good advice or comfort will help.*

me? How can I be calm when I might lose everything?" "Everything" is a vague word, and unless the world came to an end and you were the last person standing, it would be impossible to lose "everything." Still, stuck in this out-of-control space, our fears spiral and become almost fantastical.

Feeling a loss of control chips away at our confidence and, over time, results in a feeling of powerlessness that causes us to freeze up. In this way, feeling out of control is a trap that eventually prevents us from taking necessary action to get that control *back*.

SELF-CENTEREDNESS

When a crisis consumes us, causing undue stress and that out-of-control feeling, we have a tendency to become self-centered. This is partly due to the isolating factor of being in a crisis and dealing with the effects of that crisis. Your experience is your own, even if the situation is also affecting your spouse, your coworkers or your neighbors. The unknown outcome and the pain and suffering you feel are yours to fret over and endure, and the fact that other people don't seem to fully understand what you're dealing with can lead you to feel more and more alone.

Focusing on yourself—what you need, what you want, what you can do to practice self-care and, later, get your life back on track—is a healthy aspect of self-centeredness. However, when we're stuck in the self-centered trap, we rarely use this feeling to effect positive change. Instead, we use it as an excuse to react negatively to others.

We think, "What do you know about it? The crisis is happening *to me,* not you. And anyway, you would be crabby, too, if you had no idea how everything would turn out." It's as if we believe the crisis gives us a pass to behave badly—to judge others, to assign blame, to ignore the feelings of others and abandon polite behavior.

Getting stuck in the self-centered trap leads to a level of self-absorption that can only bring about negative results. In this state, it's difficult to cooperate, to seek and find a compromise and to accept our own responsibilities in the situation. How are we supposed to get our control back and reduce stress if we can't see past ourselves? It's as if we're looking for a way out of a cave with a blindfold over our eyes.

HELPLESSNESS AND VICTIMIZATION

One of the most common traps of crisis is the feeling of being a helpless victim. This trap is linked to the other traps discussed earlier—it's a snowball effect. When you are so stressed out, paralyzed by the out-of-control feeling and stuck in self-centeredness, it's the easiest thing in the world to fall into the trap of helplessness and victimization.

In this state, it's as if we've thrown our hands in the air and declared, "Why bother? This always happens to me. There's nothing I can do." We give up, believing that there is no way out of the situation—and that even if we tried it wouldn't matter, because the universe (or a person, company, and so on) is unfair and determined to make our lives a living hell.

This is another trap that is easy to fall into, because the feelings are real and also seem perfectly justifiable. Yet when we align ourselves with the victim role and act as if we truly are helpless, it makes it almost impossible for us to reduce

> *Believing you are a helpless victim*
> *is like adding gasoline to a fire.*

stress, gain control and break free from our self-centered behavior. It places the event at the forefront, adding a tremendous amount of pressure to the situation. Over time, the feeling of helplessness and victimization entraps us further, leading to overwhelming levels of stress and anxiety that could have dangerous consequences.

Believing you are a helpless victim is like adding gasoline to a fire. Everything is blown out of proportion, and a feeling of despair settles in, from which it can be difficult to break free.

FAILURE AND REJECTION

Experiencing failure and rejection is part of life. The immediate aftermath of a failure or rejection brings up a lot of emotions. You might feel angry, humiliated, nervous, afraid, sad or disappointed. These immediate reactions are manageable, however. They will pass, and you will move on. However, no longer feeling any of those negative emotions doesn't mean you've *truly* moved on from the experience.

Failure and rejection can become a trap when you carry the imprints of these experiences in your memory bank. The emotional pain you felt at the time created these imprints, and because of the painful memory, your brain wants to avoid any possibility of repeating the experience. This is why you are less likely to try again after a failure or rejection. You may feel paralyzed with fear and unable to take a chance. Or, you may intend to try again, prepare to try again, but then choke at the last minute. If the pain was great enough, you may not even *consider* trying; you may write off the goal or dream entirely and close that door forever.

Further, when you fail or are rejected, you tend to take it personally. It could be that your plan or action failed simply because it wasn't the right time or due to circumstances beyond your control. And yet you will almost always blame yourself. These feelings of self-blame have a lasting impact on your self-worth, which can shift your entire outlook on life. And, when you inevitably experience failure or rejection again—because we all do and will, and it cannot be avoided—you may perceive that experience as *proof* that you were "right" about yourself all along.

Do you see how failure and rejection can be a dangerous trap? To avoid their myriad negative repercussions, you must manage your reactions to these experiences carefully. The way you respond to failure or rejection determines whether or not you will be caught in its trap. Shatterproof Principles Two and Four will provide clarity and show you a better approach to managing failure and rejection, so you can guide yourself out of this trap before you get stuck in it.

ATTITUDE AND CHOICE

The good news about the common traps of crisis is, we *can* avoid them—or climb out of them quickly—with a simple shift in perception. Feelings of victimization and helplessness, for example, are created by the attitude we have elected to adopt. Likewise, extreme stress, feeling out of control and getting stuck in the negative side of self-centeredness are about choice—choosing to view the situation through a negative filter, which blocks out everything else.

Attitude is the way we look at something, and we make choices about how to handle a situation based on our attitude. This is good news, because we have *control* over our attitude— we can make a different choice and change it in an instant. This can seem impossible when we're caught up in crisis, which is why many people get sucked into the whirlwind of emotions and eventually get stuck in the common traps, feeling as though life has been shattered. The Seven Coping Principles are designed to help you make that important shift in perception and change your attitude quickly, enabling you to make different choices.

In this way, the Seven Coping Principles help you to become Shatterproof.

We have the choice to live in fear, anger or resentment, or to choose a different and more productive path. The Seven Coping Principles help you frame this recovery, and provide the necessary tools you need to become Shatterproof.

• • •

The emotions around crisis—even the negative ones—are perfectly normal. It is imperative that we don't cheapen them or avoid them, and that we give ourselves and others permission to experience these emotions. But it is also crucial that we know how to move on from these emotions before we get stuck. Emotions are real. They not only take a toll on the mind and on our ability to move forward, they also have a proven impact on the body.

What the mind thinks, the body believes.

When your mind is trapped in the stress of crisis—worried about potential negative outcomes, fretting over what you might have done differently, alarmed about your loss of control, stuck in a victim mentality, wondering, "Why did

> *The damage occurs when we can't seem to let go.*

this happen to me?"—it has an effect on your body. Your mind thinks life as you know it is over, or believes a catastrophe is imminent, and the body reacts as if all of that is true.

My friend Linda experienced this when the realities of owning a decorating business caused her to fall into the common traps of crisis, which in turn led to her mind and body breaking down. Eventually, though, Linda was able to turn it all around. She made a choice to change her attitude, and went from thinking, "What if I fail?" to "What if I create the best possible service-oriented decorating business?" It was a simple but powerful shift that gave her the confidence she needed to pull herself out of the traps and start working toward a positive outcome. Today, Linda operates a successful decorating business with fifteen employees and enjoys financial wealth, freedom, health, abundance and love.

Getting stuck happens when we don't have the foundational understanding of what to do next—how to shift our mindset and frame the crisis in such a way that we can move past the fear of the unknown. We're human. It's perfectly normal to get caught up in the stress, in feeling out of control, in thinking we are victims; and it's perfectly normal to get stuck focusing on ourselves. Our natural ways of reacting would work perfectly if only we could let go and move on quickly. The damage occurs when we can't seem to let go. Holding on to the resentment you feel toward a person who hurt you or toward perpetrators of actions against you, for example, all the negative feelings you've created and now hold inside constantly being fueled by revisiting and reliving the event in your mind, over and over again, is a trap.

When crisis happens, remember that we have the opportunity to grow, develop and become resistant to that same injury moving forward. Every crisis is a chance to become more than we were yesterday, to make changes and experience those turning points where we have the opportunity to take control and shape our future.

Most people will get better over time, eventually learning to let go and climb out of these traps. This process could take months, or even years. But it doesn't have to.

There is a better way. A simple way: the Seven Coping Principles.

Are you ready to get started?

Chapter 3

The First Coping Principle:
Face It Through Awareness
and Acknowledgment

Elizabeth is the proud mother of a young son, an angel and a prince who captures the heart of everyone who comes into contact with him. Elizabeth is a positive, joyful person, so bright and optimistic most people would be shocked to hear her story. You see, Nathan, her son, is autistic. For Elizabeth, raising an autistic child is a labor of love. Due to her efforts, and help from her support network and Nathan's teachers, Nathan has made good progress.

But that's not the story I meant to tell. When Nathan was just four years old, Elizabeth's mother, with whom she was very close, was diagnosed with terminal cancer. Shortly thereafter, Elizabeth discovered her husband was having an affair, which escalated until he was leaving his family for weekend escapes. She was living like a single parent. Just two months after she found out about his betrayal, he moved his belongings from the house they had shared for seven years.

Later that day, her mother died.

Elizabeth was overcome with grief, anger and pain. It was too much happening all at once—the challenges of raising an autistic child, her mother's death and her husband's abandonment when she needed him the most. Who would blame Elizabeth for going ballistic, for hating her husband, for wanting revenge in the worst possible way?

Instead, Elizabeth chose a different path. "I couldn't let myself stay in the negative emotions very long; I couldn't let them overtake me. I knew if I did, they would destroy me, and my son needed me."

Elizabeth understood the adage, "You reap what you sow." She understood that her thoughts, words and actions would be instrumental in creating her future. What good would expressing anger, or acting on it, bring her? What good would this bring her son?

"Rather than focus on all I had lost and getting even with my husband, I worked on building a positive future for Nathan," Elizabeth told me one afternoon. In the beginning, it wasn't easy. She had to deal with becoming a single mom, a legal separation, finding a new place to live and a new school for Nathan that could provide for his special needs—all while grieving the loss of her beloved mother.

During this time, she also had to deal with "friends" who were baffled by her strength and positive attitude, friends who expected her to break under the pressure of too many crises all at once. "They kept saying to me, 'Why aren't you enraged? You're too good! Why don't you get even with your ex?' So I had to detach from them, which left me with an even smaller support system."

Throughout the contentious dissolution of her marriage, Elizabeth kept her eye on the prize: a harmonious, happy environment for her and her son. She wanted Nathan to experience a loving, peaceful environment and, because of this, she was aware of her negative emotions as they popped up and redirected her attention to creating the environment she knew was best for her family.

Within months of her mother's death and her husband's betrayal, Elizabeth was able to create complete harmony for herself and her son and even in her relationship with her ex-husband, with whom she wanted her son to have a positive relationship. She created that harmony by choice. *She reaped what she sowed.*

She was able to do this because she was aware of her emotions and acknowledged that while she had no control over her circumstances—her husband's choices, her mother's death, her son's diagnosis—she could control how she reacted to those circumstances. More importantly, she could control whether or not she would allow those circumstances, or the opinions of those around her, to have an impact on the quality of her life.

Every day, in every communication with her ex, her friends, Nathan's teachers and her peers, she kept nurturing that seed of harmony. It wasn't about getting revenge. It wasn't about being angry and spewing that anger in thoughts and words. It wasn't about feeling sorry for herself or playing the victim. It wasn't about dwelling on the "unfairness" of all she had experienced and lost. It wasn't about judging her ex-husband or blaming him for her difficulties. And it wasn't about winning the next argument. It was about maintaining the harmony Elizabeth and Nathan both needed. Every day, in every way, she was aligned with her goal of creating that harmony.

If there is one Shatterproof Principle that must remain with you throughout your journey, it is the Awareness and Acknowledgment Principle. The Awareness and Acknowledgment Principle is the principle on which all of the other principles depend—without it, it is difficult to move through crisis quickly and achieve a positive outcome.

When you are aware of your emotions, thoughts, words and actions, and how they are related, you are better able to acknowledge and take responsibility for whatever situation you find yourself in. This will empower you to take control of how that situation will or won't affect you.

One single thought can change your mood instantly, bring your energy level down, initiate a downward spiral, lead to misunderstandings, cause you to make hasty decisions you may later regret and even change future outcomes. When you

> *One single thought can change*
> *your mood instantly.*

practice the Awareness and Acknowledgment Principle, you are able to recognize when you are choosing to go down a negative path. Once you are *aware* and catch yourself doing this, you can easily and quickly stop it by shifting your thinking and replacing negative thoughts with something more productive and positive.

Awareness will also give you the strength, courage and focus to step back and acknowledge that the naysayers live in a world they created for themselves, and that world is not *your* world. In Awareness, there is no desire to dwell on past events, to place blame or to try to get even. In Awareness, we acknowledge that we reap what we sow and that our thoughts, words and actions create our future circumstances. (In the Fifth Coping Principle, we will begin to take action.)

THE VERY FIRST STEP

We know all too well that symptoms are caused by an event, but sometimes we ignore the symptoms because we do not want to deal with the cause. We hope our headaches, anxiety or sleepless nights will "just go away," and bury our negative emotions about the event that caused us to develop symptoms in the first place. This is the beginning of a downward spiral that can have disastrous and long-lasting consequences.

And that is why the very first step toward coping with crisis and becoming Shatterproof is to acknowledge that you are, in fact, in a crisis. I know this may seem obvious, but as you recall, it wasn't obvious to Linda until she landed in the hospital. She had no other choice but to acknowledge that she was in a crisis—her mind and body forced it on her by generating an anxiety attack.

You may even be thinking, "Of course I know I'm in crisis. Why do you think I'm reading this book?" The truth is, most of us would not use the term "crisis" for many of the events that cause us pain or stress. It can be hard to acknowledge that a difficult string of days at work is indeed a crisis, or that a relationship with a coworker, friend or spouse is not just "a bit strained," but a crisis that warrants all of the attention that most people would devote to a crisis such as a chronic illness or an impending divorce.

My friend April did her best to avoid acknowledging that she and her husband Bob were in crisis due to his crack addiction. Bob started using drugs recreationally well into their marriage and all too quickly advanced to crack cocaine. The drug took over his life—and April's. Despite having to deal with Bob disappearing for three-day stretches, wondering if he would ever come home; despite her worries and sleepless nights; despite her own stress and the disconnect in their marriage, April refused to acknowledge that her husband was an addict.

"I was trying to avoid the whole situation. I really didn't want to have to *face* it," April told me. "I recognized how much having to face his addiction would change our lives, and I just didn't feel capable or strong enough to handle it."

April explained that her denial caused her to cover up for Bob. "I had been doing a lot of lying for him and for myself— to the kids, my parents, his parents. His mom knew something was up, but I just kept making excuses. I would tell her that he was away on trips when really he had just gone AWOL for a

> *The admission that you are in a crisis is critically important.*

couple of days. If the kids wondered why their dad was sleeping so much, I would tell them he was sick. I felt totally incapable of coping with what was happening in our lives and thinking about what the next step would be."

It wasn't until Bob disappeared for the third time that April finally acknowledged the truth and reached out for help. "Bob had been gone a couple of nights. I wouldn't let myself sleep because I had to constantly listen for him in case he came through the front door. My sister called and said, 'I know something's up.' I just lost it. I started crying uncontrollably. She said 'Hold on, I'm coming.' That night I wasn't alone—I was surrounded by family and friends, and I admitted to them what had been going on."

The admission that you are in a crisis is critically important. It is the starting line to moving through the event, and exactly what needs to happen in order to start the healing process. After April acknowledged and accepted her husband's drug addiction, she was able to make decisions and insist he go to rehab. It was the beginning of her own journey toward becoming Shatterproof.

Remembering the definition of crisis from the first chapter, it is important we understand that our acknowledgment of being in crisis is not an admission of failure. It is simply a declaration that this thing, this event, deserves your attention. Once you make this acknowledgment of crisis, you will be able to grow through it.

THE ACCUMULATION EFFECT

When we deny that we are in crisis, burying our emotions and ignoring symptoms, the stress of the situation accumulates until we reach our capacity to "just deal" and lose it. We've all seen it happen—a friend who drowns himself in too much alcohol to numb the pain, a relative who isolates herself from the world around her in order to avoid reality, a coworker who blows up over a tiny mishap unworthy of his rage.

When we refuse to acknowledge crisis, our "ability-to-maintain tank" soon becomes so full, one little drip of stress will cause it to overflow. When this happens, we often resort to poor coping mechanisms. We lash out, we self-medicate; we stop taking care of ourselves. Over time, if left buried, the overflow of stress becomes unbearable and can lead to drastic, sometimes permanent negative outcomes.

When is it that social drinking turns into alcoholism? When do prescription medications become a life-altering habit? When does anything that we do become a coping mechanism for us to get through what we are feeling? Unfortunately, these are often the questions that come up as we consider alternatives to dealing with our stress. Stress and crisis do not magically disappear. They live inside of us and, as with any emotion, feeling or thought that we try to suppress, the mind and body have the ability to ensure that at some point, we will deal with it. It may not be now, but you will deal with it; it will manifest itself at some point.

Stress is a cumulative disease. The first time we felt stress it did not kill us. We got through it to face a new day. But because of the nature of stress, its continual addition will cause us to suffer physically and emotionally. Think of yourself as a pipe. Our lives are consistently pouring new stresses into one end

Stress is a cumulative disease.

of the pipe; with each day and each crisis, more and more stress flows into that pipe. When we ignore our stress and try to pretend that it does not exist, or when we try to defer dealing with it, the pipe's exit gets blocked. Soon, obviously, the pipe begins to fill and then starts to overflow. Now each new stress increases the pressure, and at some point the pipe will burst.

Stress and the prolonged exposure to it have been proven to cause things as benign as sweating—but unfortunately, it doesn't stop there. If it did, you would have bought a stick of antiperspirant and not this book. Stress has been linked, as a major contributor, to the following disorders: high blood pressure, teeth grinding, heart problems, hair loss, change in sleep habits, susceptibility to infection, loss of sexual performance, skin problems, difficulty breathing, muscular symptoms, fatigue and sudden weight fluctuations, to name a few examples.

Often we choose not to address stress because we are too busy, or because we feel that it does not affect us. The reality is that by not dealing with the stress and crisis in our lives, we become sweaty, stiff, teeth-grinding, short-on-patience people who have difficulty breathing and sleeping well and can't perform in the bedroom... and, oh yeah, we just put on another fifteen pounds.

If you're meant to experience something, you will. The event that caused your symptoms will not just go away. You can face it now, or you can face it later... but you *will* face it. When you avoid facing it head on, negative consequences will affect your physical and mental well-being down the road.

By acknowledging crisis and becoming aware of your reactions to it (your emotions, thoughts, words and actions), you are giving yourself permission to enter this new journey, a new chapter in your life.

YOUR LIFE, THE MOVIE

Self-awareness is essential to becoming Shatterproof, but most of us are too caught up in the drama and challenges of a crisis to achieve this. We get wrapped up in worry, in other people's demands or reactions, and bounce around from one negative emotion to another.

One of the tools I use to achieve awareness is to look at the situation as if I'm watching a movie. This allows me to detach from the event, to remove myself from the real life "action" and watch it unfold like a movie on a screen.

Sit quietly. Imagine the crisis you are experiencing as a central conflict in a movie. See yourself as one of the actors on the screen, living the experience. Pay attention to how you, the character, react to situations. Take note of your emotions and how those emotions influence your thoughts, words and actions—and eventually, the outcome of the experience. Do you see how you create the ending of your movie?

You reap what you sow.

Now step back and remember that *you* are the writer, director and star of this movie. This movie is *your life*. You can change the ending. You *can* ride off into the sunset, if you simply redirect your emotions, thoughts, words and actions toward the outcome you desire. Like Elizabeth, who imagined a harmonious, peaceful home life for herself and her son, you

You can change the ending.

can create a positive outcome from whatever crisis you are experiencing now. Fear, anger, uncertainty and feelings of hopelessness and helplessness are natural reactions to crises, but they will shape how your story plays out. How could you shift your thinking and refocus your emotions to create a different outcome?

As you practice this exercise, you will notice that you can begin to detach from the event, to become an observer, and your ability to participate in effectively coping with the event will dramatically increase. This technique also helps to avoid the "fight or flight" reaction that is our natural tendency as human beings—a reaction that is not built to work with many of the modern stresses we face.

• • •

Crisis does not have to be scary. It does not have to be our scarlet letter, marking us as somehow different from the rest. In fact, if we were all to wear our crises on our sleeves, it would be most interesting to find that everyone would wear the same letter. The scarlet "C" would not be missing from anyone anywhere, regardless of status, financial situation, skin color or country of origin.

Admission that we are in a crisis does not need to be a moment of defeat. It does not need to define us or our ability to perform. It simply needs to be a recognition that now is the time to devote the energy to addressing this issue. It is an opportunity to grow and develop on some level, and the chance we have to move through what we are experiencing and perhaps live a life with whatever the gift is that we will inevitably find in this crisis, if we allow ourselves to look.

For many, it is difficult to give consideration to a brighter tomorrow. The loss of a fortune, a loved one, a job or a family home often seems like the darkest moment. But I can promise you that tomorrow the earth will still rotate around the sun. Life will go on, and no matter how dark the situation, no matter how much you wish it never happened or that it would all just go away, tomorrow is a new day: one filled with hope, new possibilities and the chance to live a life full of joy and optimism.

The turning point for April began when she finally acknowledged her situation, when she faced it. From that moment forward, she was able to face every other disappointment or challenge that came up in relation to Bob's addiction. It wasn't an easy ride, but every step helped her to grow stronger. With help from her family, she focused on her kids and her own healing. She gained confidence in her abilities and learned how to detach from Bob's situation. April now knows she can stand on her own two feet and that she can survive anything.

Over the course of four years, Bob got treatment for his disease and, though he experienced trials and setbacks, he slowly got himself back and into recovery. He stayed in contact with April, and life did go on. Not only did they come to a peace in their relationship, they were actually able to reconcile. Years after they separated, they realized that they still loved each other and wanted to be together. And because they had learned how to live independently, because they had weathered all of the stressful events and come out the other side better able to cope, set boundaries and ask for and get what they needed, they knew that they could try again and be successful. Today, they are happily married! More importantly, April now knows she is more than capable of handling anything that comes her way—good, bad or terrible—whether Bob is there or not. She has become Shatterproof.

All of this begins with the first Shatterproof Principle: Awareness and Acknowledgment. Acknowledging you are in crisis, and becoming aware of your emotions about that crisis, allows you to access a second level of awareness, one that brings us back to the surprising definition of crisis:

That a turning point in your life is also a real possibility for something different and better.

1. Have you acknowledged that you are in crisis or in a stressful situation? If not, please take a moment to do so.

2. Examine your mindset toward the event you are experiencing. Ask yourself, "How am I feeling right now?" Become aware of your emotions, as they are the seeds for the world you are creating.

3. Do you find yourself trying to win the next argument or get the last word?

4. Do you find yourself spewing anger in thoughts and words? If so, ask yourself, "How do these thoughts, words or actions serve me in creating a better environment and future for myself, my family and my loved ones?"

5. If you find yourself thinking negatively and letting your emotions take you down a negative path, ask yourself, "How does this serve me, my loved ones, and my colleagues?"

6. We will explore this further in Chapter 5, but for now, ask yourself, "How will these emotions serve me?"

7. Imagine your life as a movie. Watch the events play out, noticing how your emotions, thoughts, words and actions influence the outcome.

Note: I created a free workbook for you, so that you can answer these and other questions and track your progress in one place. You'll also find helpful exercises. To download your free copy of *The Shatterproof Workbook*, go to shatterproofbook.com/resources.

Chapter 4

The Second Coping Principle: The Wake-Up Call— Accept and Embrace It

W e're giving you two quarters. It's January now, so you have until the end of June and if you don't hit your numbers by then, you're out." Sitting across from the president and vice president of the company, I was in total shock. Less than a year ago, they thought I could do no wrong; they had recruited me from a sales position in the Calgary office to management in Toronto, offering me five percent ownership in the company for which I had produced stellar results. Now they were just months away from kicking me to the curb.

Somehow, I made it through the rest of the meeting and all the way to my car before I let myself feel the full effects of the blow my superiors had just dealt me. I knew they weren't happy, but this was too much! I'd moved my entire family to Toronto, given the company everything I had… or had I?

As I gripped the wheel of the car and tried to control my breathing, I recalled the meeting I'd had with the president back in August. "This office is not performing well, and we need to make a change," he had said. This was not news to me. Toronto is the New York City of Canada—there was far more competition, there were more distractions, and I had more difficulty keeping people focused. It was a culture shock for me; everything was different. Every day I worked my tail off and still could not get the results expected of me.

While I knew we were struggling, that I was struggling, I fully expected us to work together to come up with a strategy to turn things around. Instead, I was demoted. "We're moving you back down to sales, Conrad."

The demotion had stopped me cold and started the beginning of a slump from which I couldn't get out. It seemed as though I had failed—not just at this job, but also at my entire career. With no tools for coping with stress, no steps to

> *When you choose resistance, you get nothing.*

handle crises, I fell easily into the common traps of crisis (see Chapter Two). I played the victim and blamed everyone but myself for my predicament. My favorite phrase was, "Why is this happening to *me*?" As if the universe had purposely saddled me with a poor economy, and the wrong coworkers and the wrong client accounts. And those feelings of being trapped led to the worst slump I'd ever experienced, which, of course, only made things worse.

Now, sitting in my car, faced with the very real prospect of losing my job, I was desperate to make a change.

Two conversations helped me do that. First, I talked with my wife Carol, who listened as I debriefed her about the meeting and expressed my concerns, and then simply said, "Well, if you are going to leave anyway, why not leave on your own terms? Just make it work."

She was right, of course, but if the circumstances that held me back hadn't changed, how would tomorrow be any different?

Soon after that I ran into my friend Mel, a man who had thrived despite his own personal crises, and I shared my predicament with him. Like Carol, he listened attentively and then gave me a simple, yet powerful response: "Conrad, are you going to play on the court or sit in the stands?"

It was then that I realized that in blaming everyone and everything, I *had been* sitting in the stands. It was as if I were pointing out the players' errors and complaining about losing while refusing to just get off my butt and get in the game. In that moment, I understood that my resistance to the demotion had brought on my slump. I had been so paralyzed by that crisis, I had let myself get stuck in a self-centered spiral of helplessness and loss of control.

Once I decided to accept the situation I was in and embrace it as an opportunity (get in the game in order to rise above the situation, or at least leave on my own terms), it was as if the fog lifted and I could see clearly. For the first time in months I did not say, "Why me?"

Instead I said, "I'm going to stay in this and figure it out." I shifted my thinking from a position of defeat (a common trap) and adopted an attitude of fighting back to conquer the challenge I was given.

That was my wake-up call. I had the choice to remain a spectator in the stands. Or I could get back in the game with the mindset and commitment to win. I chose to get back in the game.

As you move toward becoming Shatterproof, the Second Coping Principle is the first step in moving forward out of the trap, or slump or black hole you've found yourself in as a result of crisis. It's the first step because only when we accept that we are in crisis—and embrace the opportunity for growth, for positive change—can we actually do that thing that right now may seem impossible: Climb out of these traps, slumps and holes and see the light of day.

IF YOU LET IT BREAK YOU, YOU WON'T GET THE "BREAK-THROUGH"!

We're often ill-equipped to take a positive approach to getting through a crisis or setback, because we're afraid that we will have to make some changes and some difficult decisions. The last thing we want to do is face the possibility that we may lose some of the comforts and pleasures to which we've become accustomed. When we're afraid that we will have to give something up, it is because we fail to see what we may gain in return.

> *We're afraid to give something up because we fail to see what we may gain in return.*

Have you ever renovated a room in your house? Is it possible to make it through a renovation without dealing with disruption, loss of comfort and mess? No, it isn't. Is it possible to go through a renovation without having to destroy and tear down what exists? Nope. Is it possible to renovate and improve without experiencing change? Not possible, no matter how well you plan, or how hard you try. Yet if you avoid all this, you'll never get that beautiful new kitchen, or that elegant master bathroom, or whatever new room you've been dreaming about. When you resist all this, you end up living in the same old house you've always lived in, a house that may genuinely need improvements for safety, better energy efficiency, ease or quality of living or even financial gain.

When you choose resistance, you get nothing. When you choose to accept and embrace your situation, you get something you can't buy or manufacture—you get the possibility for growth, expansion and real, lasting transformation.

Only by accepting and embracing the situation can we open ourselves to the possibilities of adopting change, which allows our knowledge, horizons and outlook on life to expand. Only by accepting and embracing the situation will we be able to see things that we weren't able to see before.

You can only see what you understand, and your understanding is limited by the size of the "box" you choose to play in. We all have a different set of qualities, experiences and resources: genetic makeup, where we grew up, family of origin, education, obligations, challenges and perceived and real limitations. All of this is part of your box. But if you are experiencing a crisis, you have the opportunity to expand your box, thereby expanding your potential to grow in all facets of life.

Think of crisis as your personal educator, your teacher, your personal coach. By accepting and embracing the crisis, you open yourself to growth, to discovering who you are.

Without crisis, without setbacks and hurdles, how would we learn? How would we evolve?

A crisis will either break you, or you'll have a "breakthrough"! You alone have the power and control to choose which outcome you want.

FINDING THE GIFT

The idea that there is a gift, a lesson, a turning point—or something that will ultimately make us better people—in moving forward through a crisis can be difficult to accept. Without fail, each person I interviewed before writing this book told me that they gained something from the crisis they experienced. For some it was a better understanding or a lesson learned; for others, it was the discovery of a new interest or mission in life. Some people built stronger relationships, or found the courage to become who they always wanted to be.

And in every case, these people came through their crises knowing that they could handle almost anything—something they had not previously believed to be true.

In this step, it is important that you do not get hung up on the idea of what that gift will be. It has been said that hindsight is 20/20, and in the case of a crisis that is absolutely true. Often the gift in a crisis is not fully understood for some time after the crisis has passed. In a major crisis, like a divorce or financial setback, it can at first be difficult to see what could possibly be taken from the event to make us better. We may not realize how we've changed until well after we've conquered the crisis, and it might even take the keen observation of a friend or family member to help us see it all. No matter what the gift is, how "big" or "small," or when you receive it (or realize it), the fact remains that there is always a gift.

When I discuss this principle, some people will inevitably say, "There is no possible good that could come from what I experienced." For those people, I always share my personal stories and those of the people I interviewed for this book—people who lost children, people who experienced terrible

> *A crisis will either break you, or you'll have a "break-through"!*

crimes; people who, like me, lost the ones closest to their heart. All of these people, no matter how difficult their setbacks, no matter how tragic their circumstances will, without hesitation, be able to tell you what they gained from the experience.

Finding good in our experiences is not inherent in many people. It requires work, it requires a paradigm shift away from feelings of victimization and helplessness and it requires a true shift in how we search out the good in our crisis. From now on, when an unexpected and difficult event comes your way, face it by saying:

"I may not see it clearly now, but in this crisis, there is opportunity. I will grow from this and I will become stronger. I will find that this gift will be precious to me and will help me on the road to becoming who I want to become. It may not be easy, but it will be worth it."

PERFECT IS NOT IDEAL

We all strive to achieve a perfect environment for ourselves, filled with all the comforts and pleasures we can imagine.

We want perfect homes, with perfect spouses and perfect kids. We want perfect work conditions, perfect friendships, perfect everything. Now, you may disagree that you strive for perfection, but the truth is, whether you use the word "perfect" or not, we are all striving for our own best life and we perceive that "best life" to be free from conflict and "negative" experiences. We want green lights all the way, a smooth ride toward a destination that is easy to get to. Who wouldn't?

And yet this imaginary conflict-free, challenge-free environment is not ideal, because it does not offer the opportunity for continued growth.

Though I can't find the original article, I remember reading about trees growing in the "perfect" environmental conditions of a biosphere. While the biosphere was designed to help all living things achieve optimal growth, scientists found that trees would often flourish for a short time and then die prematurely. Why? Because their "perfect" environmental conditions did not give the trees a chance to grow strong roots. Eventually, the trees would fall over, unable to support their own weight.

The trees died in the biosphere because as they grew, they did not experience any environmental challenges that help other trees endure the forces that may act upon them—even gravity!

We, much like these trees, do not flourish under perfect conditions. When everything is perceived as perfect, we do not look for opportunities to change or grow.

From the time we learn to walk, we are trained to take the path of least resistance. Yet as we grow and develop as people, as we learn to build up tolerance to change and crisis, and as we plow forward regardless of what we experience, we discover that it is through adversity that we grow. It is through our challenges that we receive the gift of depth of character, which transforms us from being like the pampered trees we find in a biosphere to the weather-hardened survivors that we can become.

IF NOTHING ELSE...

The gift of crisis may not be anything so glamorous as a spiritual awakening, a new love or a profound understanding of human nature. Still, there is always a gift.

If you receive nothing else from this experience, you will, without a doubt, gain *resiliency*. As you move through challenges, your ability to tolerate new challenges increases exponentially, so that each time a crisis comes up, you are better able to handle it. You know this works—just look back at your earlier life events or crises. If you had to face something similar again, would you be better prepared to handle it? Would it fill you with as much dread? Would it take over your life, or would you be able to use the experiences you gained in the past as teaching tools to tackle the crisis at hand?

When my coworker and good friend Rob was fired from his job he took it very hard. "I was depressed and angry. When the news came I was shocked, because we were told that we hit the target and we were all safe. Quite frankly, I felt betrayed. I went through a lot of fear, wondering what I was going to do."

Rob was older and hadn't had to hunt for a new job in quite some time. He was worried that he would make a wrong turn, or would be unable to compete. He struggled, trying to navigate the job market and deal with his own shattered sense of value. He questioned himself and his worth—who would want to hire an older guy who had been fired from his last job?

Eventually, Rob did find a new job. But that's not the gift he found in the crisis. The gift was a newfound confidence—a resiliency. "If something like that happened again, I would be able to walk into a new job much quicker. I discovered I do have a lot to bring to this industry and I had always questioned

> *Resiliency gives you a quiet sense of confidence.*

that. Now, I think I would be able to handle it much easier. I wouldn't be as panicked, that's for sure. That sense of value, in myself, is something I take with me. I know now that I have the ability to make it work, no matter what happens."

Resiliency gives you a quiet sense of confidence, born of knowing that you've been through difficult times before and that they don't last forever.

· · ·

Choosing to accept and embrace crisis allows you to move forward—to heal, find peace of mind and grow. Without this step, you may get stuck in the common traps and delay the inevitable promise of working through a crisis: the gift.

After I received the news that I would be let go if I did not dramatically improve my numbers, I was faced with the reality that I had let my resistance to the previous demotion land me in a slump. Only after I accepted and embraced the reality of the situation was I able to turn things around. Recall that I was given two quarters—six months—to make it work. I took baby steps, made a plan and took action every day. When the six months was up, all the small accomplishments added up to enough deals to ensure I could keep my job.

Within a year, I was making million-dollar deals. The numbers I cranked were phenomenal. The president and vice president had implemented a bonus incentive that promised twenty- to forty-percent commission if we reached crazy high numbers. I broke through their highest numbers and garnered the highest commission. That year, I was named Salesman of the Year.

It is when you accept and embrace the crisis that the momentum changes. Even if your first attempts don't work out perfectly—mine certainly didn't—you will at least feel as though you're accomplishing *something*. If you keep taking baby steps, you will spot new opportunities where previously you saw nothing, and positive change will start to happen.

> *It is when you accept and embrace the crisis that the momentum changes.*

Every small deal that I made built my confidence to the point where I could get the big numbers. But it wasn't the forty-percent commission that propelled me forward; it was the fact that I was so afraid I would end up back in the slump. I never wanted to feel stuck, despondent and frustrated in that way again.

After this crisis, accepting and embracing change was ingrained in me—because I saw the result of *not* doing that, of resisting reality and keeping my head in the sand. I made a vow never to be paralyzed by crisis again.

If, right now, you don't know how it will be possible to find the gift in whatever crisis you are experiencing, don't worry.

It will come. As you complete the Seven Coping Principles to becoming Shatterproof, you will find it. Not knowing what your "break-through" will be is taking a leap of faith, for sure. But what else can you do? Your alternative is to resist. What will you gain by resisting? You'll likely get stuck and gain nothing.

The only way out of this is through acceptance of the crisis, and embracing the opportunity for newfound clarity or growth, more confidence or knowledge, closer relationships and a deeper sense of spirituality, or, if nothing else, resilience.

1. Remember a crisis from the past. In what way(s) was this experience a gift?

2. If you were faced with a similar crisis again, how would you handle it differently?

3. How could you apply this to your current situation?

4. What are some of the possible gifts you could gain from the crisis you are currently experiencing?

5. What do you most *want* to gain from this experience?

6. What would it mean to you to gain resiliency, to have a "break-through?"

Here is an Accepting and Embracing statement you can use to help you move forward with this Second Coping Principle:

"I don't know or understand why this is happening, but I do accept that this is a necessary experience for me to live through. I am willing to learn and to be open to whatever knowledge and wisdom this experience will teach me that is absolutely essential for my growth, evolution and life purpose. As difficult as this may be, I will embrace it and make the best of this situation knowing there's a higher purpose, despite the limitations of what I'm able to see or understand at this stage."

Note: I created a free workbook for you, so that you can answer these and other questions and track your progress in one place. You'll also find helpful exercises. To download your free copy of *The Shatterproof Workbook*, go to shatterproofbook.com/resources.

Chapter 5

The Third Coping Principle: Navigating the Worst-Case Scenario—The "Now What?" Stage

After I got the phone call informing me that nearly all of my fortune and retirement security were potentially gone, I went through the first two Coping Principles quickly. Through regular practice, being aware, acknowledging my situation and accepting its reality had become subconsciously built-in as part of my nature. So I faced our financial crisis head-on. It was a major shake-up in our comfortable lifestyle—a shake-up I accepted and embraced. What other choice did I have?

The result of that initial phone call was inconclusive; Carol and I knew that our money was at risk, but not to what extent.

In the days and weeks that followed, we speculated about what could have happened and what might happen in the future. We were knee-deep in rumors, but no answers could be found. After a few weeks, it became apparent that there would not be an easy fix. One day we would hear that there was a "good chance of recovering everything," and the next we would be told that everything was gone. We realized we might never find out how much of our money was gone, let alone get it back.

The weeks after the phone call that changed everything were a roller coaster ride. The Securities and Exchange Commission (SEC) got involved, and a bankruptcy trustee was appointed. Anonymous sources caused massive confusion—investigators followed up on claims that these sources knew where the money was, only to discover the existence of more than three hundred offshore accounts set up by the financial experts we trusted. As for who was responsible, there was finger pointing in all directions. Other investors formed groups for potential lawsuits. All of this was taking an emotional toll on Carol and me. Something had to change quickly. We needed to get off of the roller coaster and figure out how to regain some control.

I was in the "now what?" stage and, for me, this represented an opportunity to explore all possibilities, including my vision for the future, my goals and possible outcomes for this specific crisis situation. One possible outcome was the worst-case scenario. In this case, I had to assume that the money we had invested was gone.

For me, it wasn't just about imagining the worst-case scenario; it was about taking care of my family and our affairs *as if* the worst-case scenario would come to pass. In order to be able to turn the page and start a new chapter, I had to assume that we had less than twenty percent of our savings left, and if we were to recoup any of the money we lost, it would be a bonus. From the moment I adopted this attitude, I never wavered from it.

Why didn't I hold on to a different, more positive outcome? Consider the alternative. I could continue to live day in and day out on the roller coaster ride, getting entrenched in the drama of trying to figure out what had happened and how to get our money back. Waiting for a happy ending to this story would keep me in the negative space, fueled by resentment, with constant reminders of the loss. Steeped in anger, frustration, fear, anxiety, worry, sadness and depression, I would continue to feel victimized, helpless and out of control. Why would I want to live that way? I wanted off the ride.

To be clear, choosing to operate as if the worst-case scenario would come to pass did not mean that I did not think about the crisis or deal with it. There were aspects of the investigation to which I needed to attend. But I did not let my involvement in the situation consume me. I did not allow myself to stay in the negative space for any length of time.

At this point you may be thinking, "This is easier said than done." For some that may be true. For those who learn and practice the Seven Coping Principles, it *can* become that easy.

> *You too have a choice as to where to direct your attention.*

Where we choose to direct our attention can make a huge impact on our ability to thrive during a crisis. The power of the Principles is, when practiced, they will help you redirect your attention toward what you *can* control.

In the end, it took eight years to resolve the crisis, and the money returned to us was pennies on the dollar! What if I had lived on that roller coaster ride for eight long years? I would have become a basket case. My life would have been in a complete shambles had I chosen to take that path.

And that is the key: choice. You too have a choice as to where to direct your attention. Will you hold on to the past and worry about the future in the hope that you will have the outcome you believe is best for you? Or will you learn to live the best life you can, even if the worst happens?

WORST-CASE SCENARIO BOUNDARIES

Before we begin considering your worst-case scenario, we need to set some boundaries and context. In the beginning, we have a tendency to allow our "what ifs" to turn into wildly unlikely and even humorous scenarios that warrant no attention at all. It is important that we stay focused on reality, rather than let our imaginations run away with us. Otherwise, this exercise is fueled by even more negativity.

My worst-case scenario was completely realistic—there was a decent chance we would never see eighty percent of our investments again. But what if I had allowed my mind to spiral with ridiculous "worst-case" outcomes, such as:

- "My friends and family will see me as a loser and disown me."
- "I'll never be able to go anywhere or have any fun, ever again!"
- "My wife will leave me and I'll be alone."
- "I'll have to get a job I despise and work long hours."
- "I'll have to work until I'm very old, and I won't be able to take care of myself, and I'll end up living on the streets. I'll die during a cold spell on a winter night, and no one will find me until the spring thaw!"

As we discussed earlier, the climax of all crises is that moment when there is an abundance of unknowns—so many things could and might happen that our minds race through scenario after scenario, playing out often wildly exaggerated possibilities. It is in these moments when we can lose control *to our crisis*. It's as if our crisis owns us, and that's when the feelings of hopelessness and being out of control show up. So focus on reality, and let's move forward.

Every crisis and stressful situation usually has one worst-case scenario. You'll become aware of it when it seems you're about to lose something. In order to become Shatterproof, you need to consider what it would be like if what you're afraid to lose *were* gone, and how you would handle that situation. You need to know that you can and will survive the experience. So if you're afraid you might lose your job, your home, your investments, your spouse through separation or divorce, your health or perhaps something you own, your worst-case scenario is that you will lose it—and if you *don't* lose it, it will be a bonus.

In this mindset, you are now forced to direct your attention to the realm of possibilities and opportunities this outcome could provide; the potential impact the loss would have on your life, your work, your health and your family; and the potential ways you could navigate this crisis if the worst-case scenario did come to pass.

Another way to look at it is to approach it like playing a game of chess. To win, you not only have to look at your present move, but also potential future moves; and you must also consider the moves your opponent might make. At a more advanced level, you implement various strategies that you've visualized to outwit your opponent and win the game. Looking at your worst-case scenario and its impact on your life, you then look for various possibilities and opportunities—your next move and your future moves—to navigate the crisis as best you can.

Looking at the worst case from a high-level perspective, you don't need to come up with all the details. Just work on discovering the possible solutions to various scenarios you find yourself in. The details will be worked out under the Fifth Coping Principle.

IT COULD BE WORSE

Regardless of the situation you're in right now, your worst-case scenario could always be worse. This is an important perspective to adopt. I know this may seem difficult to accept, but stay with me for a moment. Once I adopted the mindset that our money was gone, my focus changed from trying to figure out what had happened and how to get our money back to figuring out what I needed to do to keep our family afloat without the money. I was considering my next move and my future moves as I thought about our income, expenses and where we stood financially.

At the time, we had mortgages on two luxury homes, leases on two high-end vehicles and other financial obligations. The bottom line was, considering the worst-case scenario, we could no longer afford the lifestyle we had been living. It was time to make some difficult decisions and act on those decisions quickly. I knew we had to reduce our living expenses and find new sources of revenue. And we had to get our hands on whatever money we did have left in other investments so we could get some control back.

During this time, I frequently told myself, "It could be worse. A lot worse." We weren't totally wiped out. We came from humble beginnings, and I knew we could manage happily with less because we had been happy with very little before. It would be an adjustment at first, but it was something we could easily overcome. In my early forties, I was still young enough to earn an income, so I thought, "I still have time to make this back somehow."

Here's why adopting the worst-case scenario mindset and acknowledging that your situation could be worse is so important: When you look ahead, mindful of the fact that your worst is not the worst it could be, you stop feeling sorry for yourself and getting stuck in the past, which you can't change or control.

My friend Mel is like a cat; I like to say he's been blessed with nine lives. When he was nineteen years old, he worked as a packer (also known as a paver) on a road construction crew and suffered a terrible accident. In his recovery his view of the world changed.

"It was Friday, and the guys I worked with were headed to the big city, to the bar. I wanted to work overtime because I was going to school. So I was alone, driving my packer back and forth, packing gravel into the tar," Mel recounted to me.

"I was going up an incline and got too close to the shoulder, and the packer, which weighs twenty tons, got too close to the edge. The edge gave way, sucking me into the ditch and almost severing my arm. When I rolled back, the packer rolled and landed on top of me. I was pinned underneath the engine with the wheels on top of my hips, facing the sky with hot antifreeze dripping on me."

Because it wasn't unusual to see construction equipment parked for the night at the side of the road, none of the people driving by thought anything of the packer in the ditch. After three hours the radiator started to overheat, which was a blessing because it caught the attention of a person driving by.

Mel said, "He came down into the ditch and couldn't believe that I was under the packer. I asked him to get some help, and he went and got a grader and put the blade under the packer. All of the farmers in the area—there must have been fifty to a hundred of them—drove their trucks over to the accident site and shined their lights on the packer so that the rescue team had enough light to pull me out."

At the hospital, Mel was rushed to intensive care. His arm was broken, and because the doctors were worried about blood clots traveling to his heart or brain, they wanted to amputate his legs. In the end, they did not amputate, but Mel was in the hospital for nine months, paralyzed below the waist for the first seven. And because he had severed the nerves in one arm, he only had one good arm left.

"In the beginning it was a depressing time because I was paralyzed and I was dealing with a bit of self-pity. But then I looked around me and realized that there were people there who were worse off," Mel explained.

"There was this older guy, probably in his sixties, who'd had both of his legs severed at the knee. He said to me, 'Mel, you either pick it up and have a good attitude or you're going to be like that guy across the hall who is wallowing in misery and self-pity and doesn't want to do anything.' That's when I learned that if I didn't have a positive attitude, I could be stuck in the hospital for a long, long time.

"I realized that I might not recover and walk again. But I had also met some great people who were in wheelchairs, and I knew it was all in their attitude. You're not handicapped unless you say you're handicapped."

That's when things turned around for Mel. Realizing it could be worse and considering the worst-case scenario—being stuck in a wheelchair for the rest of his life—inspired him to not only change his attitude, but to consider the small possibility of walking again. "Even though rehab hurt like hell, I began to think there was a reason for physical therapy. I began to visualize the realm of possibilities. I made a decision and set a goal for myself: to walk into the prom with my girlfriend."

Having faced his worst-case scenario that he might not walk again and observed people in a similar position, Mel realized that he would be okay. He went from feeling self-pity to feeling lucky. When I asked him what he learned from the experience, he said, "It taught me that even though I was in a bad situation, it could have been worse. I learned about myself, my survival skills, a lot about my strength—internal and physical."

A little less than one year later, after putting in a great deal of effort and enduring pain and discomfort, Mel was rewarded: He was able to walk into the prom with his girlfriend.

You will gain power and control from looking at the worst-case scenario and navigating through it, examining it, *seeking the realm of possibilities,* knowing that it could always be worse—every crisis or difficult moment you're in could always be worse—and by shifting your mindset and adopting a positive attitude. The instant you make the choice to see things this way, you're already starting to heal. You are already putting yourself in forward motion, putting yourself in a position to succeed; you can't help but achieve some level of success.

WHEN THE WORST-CASE SCENARIO BECOMES REALITY

I've often been asked, "Conrad, how was it possible to navigate through the worst-case scenario when you found out that your wife Carol was dying?"

Navigating through the worst-case scenario when the worst case is that someone you love is going to die, is going to be taken away from you, when you know you're going to lose this person—this is no easy task to face and experience. However, you still have control and power to choose which attitude you plan to adopt and where to direct your attention.

Within one week of receiving the result of the MRI, going through a biopsy and getting the prognosis from the oncologist, we knew there would not be a happy ending. My worst-case scenario was that Carol was going to die within twelve to eighteen months. As much as I didn't want this outcome, as much as I wanted to save her, as much as I wanted to take her place and take away her suffering, I couldn't. As much as I hated the fact that for over seven years we were unaware of the severity of her situation, and no one had been able to diagnose this cancer earlier, there was nothing I could do, control or influence that would change the result of what Carol was experiencing. Nothing!

I realized that this was Carol's journey and destiny, and that as much as the affection, love and attachment we shared were part of my journey, this was about her and not me.

Despite not having the ability or control to change the result of the worst-case scenario, I chose to be the best that I could be to support, to help, to console and to be completely and consciously present in every way possible. I chose to make Carol's journey and transition as spiritual, joyous and comfortable as possible. Choosing this approach allowed me to heal throughout the journey and after she died.

I never wavered from that mindset and was with her every step of her final journey. Looking back, we experienced some of the most beautiful, loving and deeply touching moments of our entire life together at that time. Carol died four months after her diagnosis. From outside the situation, anyone would look at our experience and assume it was pure hell. But it wasn't. Though difficult, experiencing the journey fully present with Carol proved to be one of the most beautiful, powerful and rewarding four months of my life.

So how can you possibly embrace the notion that it could be worse when your loved one is dying? The four-month journey could have been so much worse. Carol's quality of life was diminishing rapidly after the first month of radiation and chemo treatments. Once her quality of life was gone, she could have lived for months and months, but didn't.

During this time, I saw and met other spouses in the hospital who were going through the same experience with their loved ones. For some, quality of life was gone but they remained alive for over twelve months. I didn't want that for Carol. The various medications she was taking had horrendous potential side effects; using them over a prolonged period would perforate her stomach, causing her to bleed internally. That could have happened, but didn't.

You see, Carol could have suffered from pain and experienced various negative side effects that didn't happen. Her pain and her pain medicine were very well managed and controlled. It could have been so much worse and so much more difficult.

Carol's attitude in accepting her journey was profoundly inspiring. I don't think there's anything more heroic for any of us than to accept our destiny in facing death. She was truly heroic in her strength and courage. So you can see how easily I could think of a thousand ways that it could have been a lot worse.

FINDING THE BEST ASPECT OF THE WORST THING

The power of acknowledging the worst-case scenario is not only expressed in the ways it helps you navigate a crisis; it is also present in the opportunity it gives you to ask, while going through the experience: "What are the opportunities here to see the benefit of what I have just gone through?" It's being aware of what takeaways and rewards come with this experience.

An exercise you can try is to imagine your "higher self" sitting above you, saying, "I'm going to counsel myself on all the opportunities that exist." When you approach a worst-case scenario this way, it gives you a different view that before, you probably would not have allowed yourself to see. And it presents you with a whole bucketful of opportunities. Depending on the situation, this may be an opportunity to start over—a clean slate allowing you the freedom to explore and go in a new direction in your life, one from which you might otherwise shy away.

Imagine losing a child in your arms because she drowned in your pool. How can you possibly navigate through the worst-case scenario under this circumstance, when the worst case has already occurred—your daughter dying from drowning? It's hard to think of something more unfair, unjust, incomprehensible, devastating and heartbreaking.

This happened to a close friend of mine, Chris, whom I deeply respect and admire for what he had to endure and what he has become. Here's an excerpt from Chris's story:

"I remember waking up the day after it happened, and we had a guest bedroom downstairs; all of our family was there and everybody was trying to be helpful and hustling around and doing their thing, and one of the people that had come was my sister-in-law, who happened to have a daughter that was just weeks different in age from mine. I remember waking up hearing that voice—that little girl, squeaky girl voice. And I can remember my heart leaping like it was all a dream and then seeing Kate come running by the door and thinking, 'Oh, it wasn't a dream; it's real.'

"I remember waking up the day afterwards, and I remember this realization that I had a decision to make, and that it was my decision to make, and that no one could make it for me, and that no one could take that decision away from me and that was the decision of, 'How am I going to cope?' And I realized that I had reached the end of the road that I had been walking on and that I could turn right or I could turn left.

"Turning right meant accepting what had happened and continuing forward in strength, and being there as a force for good in my family and embracing the faith that I had been raised with and the knowledge that I have of what comes next; or I could choose the left turn, which would mean being angry with God and angry with the world—why did this happen to me?—and play the 'why me?' card. Basically just play the pity card and feel bad for myself, start self-medicating and head down what I knew would be a long and dark path.

"So I remember that decision and lying there in bed. It was a very quiet morning and sunny, and you could hear all the birds outside. And I distinctly remember, there was this really clear moment amongst the anguish that was one where I realized that I have to choose. And I just made the conscious decision that it wasn't going to be the end. There would be a lot more to live for. I had two children and a wife that needed me desperately, and I had a lot of life to live.

"While it was a terrible thing that had happened, I would take whatever good that I could take from that experience—whatever positive could be excavated out of that train wreck—and share that experience with as many people as I could to help people understand that these things happen—and who knows why they happen, and who knows how the universe chooses who. They happen, but at the end of the day, I don't think anyone would trade with anybody else. We all get dealt the hand we get dealt and we all have the opportunity to choose our next move.

"So that's what I remember. It isn't a wish I would wish on my most dire enemy, and yet I have always wished that every person, every parent, would have the opportunity to look at their children the way that you look at your children after you've lost a child, because ever since that day four years ago I've never looked at my children the same…"

For Chris, one of the opportunities that existed for him when he lost his daughter was being forced to look at his life. This gave him a chance to get out of a business that he had no business being in and go in a new direction, and to focus on the things that mattered most in his life. He was at a crossroads. He had to make a choice. He could have easily gone down the dark path of self-destruction as a victim, feeling helpless and hopeless, and no one would have blamed him for it.

Instead, Chris recommitted to being a better father to his existing children and a better husband to his wife. There's not a day that goes by that he doesn't think about his daughter; but he harnesses the beautiful memories of his daughter to transform his own life, allowing him to live more vibrantly and be present with his children and his wife, knowing how precious and fragile life is and how much he appreciates every passing day with them.

OTHER USES FOR THE WORST-CASE SCENARIO COPING PRINCIPLE

The Worst-Case Scenario Coping Principle can also be used when you are confronted with a difficult decision. Perhaps you're at a crossroads in your career, opportunities are being presented to you and you're unsure about which way to go. Go through the above steps and also see what the worst-case scenario of each choice is.

For example, I used this principle when deciding if I should leave my present job or go with a new start-up opportunity.

The risk in going to the start-up was extremely high. But the potential reward was equally high. So we had to examine what our worst-case scenario would be if I went to the start-up. We were also contemplating investing our money (a good chunk of our retirement savings) into the start-up, which made the stakes even higher.

After examining the worst-case scenario, we knew with confidence what decision we should make. We understood the risk. We knew we could navigate the risk. For us, it meant that we were going to invest and live off of part of our savings for a while, since this start-up didn't pay much at first. We were able to look at how this would work for one year and expected that after that year, I would know if the start-up had the potential to become something or not. If it didn't work out, I would have to find another job, and we would lose all the money we had invested in the new venture.

You can be the director of your healing.

Even knowing the downside, we saw an upside to this potential failure. I would gain invaluable experience. At that particular moment in our lives, we were both willing to live with the worst-case scenario if it did happen to go that way. It was a calculated risk that we examined carefully. Well, in our case, the high risk we took paid off handsomely, and we were able to accumulate a great deal of wealth. But we didn't know how it would turn out when making the decision. After we did this exercise and made the decision, I was able to concentrate one hundred percent on the business. I was confident while attempting to make this start-up a success, since we had already, proactively, developed a plan that we both accepted if it didn't work out.

· · ·

Now most times, the worst case you've imagined never occurs. This exercise allows you to prepare proactively for the worst-case scenario. If you can see yourself navigating the worst realistic outcome imaginable, with possible options, solutions and work-arounds, the impact and pressure that come with the "unknown" factor will be taken out of the equation. The real impact and climax of a crisis are not the event itself, but the thing that comes after the event. It's called "not knowing what's going to happen next." That is the "climax" and scariest part of any crisis.

Although most times the worst-case scenario never happens, you still need to prepare for it and be willing to accept the fact that you may be forced to live through it. And sometimes you need to be proactive and make tough decisions,

> *No matter what you have had to endure,*
> *tomorrow the sun will come up.*

so that you're not waiting for the situation to get completely out of control, to the point where others gain control and decide for you.

You can be the director of your healing. You can be in charge of your future. You can control what happens now and, although you may not believe it right now, you can get through this, no matter what happens. One of the common threads between those who have experienced tragedy in their lives is a feeling that their worlds stopped. At some point it was difficult for them to believe that tomorrow the sun would come up, that the world would continue to move forward. They felt such overwhelming grief and sadness that it was hard to imagine how the world around them could continue to operate as if nothing had happened.

If there is one thing I can give you in this chapter, it is this: No matter what you have had to endure, tomorrow the sun will come up. Tomorrow *will* be a new day, filled with hours in which you can make progress, heal and move forward. On that day, if not today, you will be able to make a decision to do what is necessary to heal, and if you follow this plan and trust in it, you *can* get through this.

You are stronger than you believe. You can endure more than you know. Take control, be courageous and move to a better, healthier, more productive place.

Chapter 6

The Fourth Coping Principle: Free Your Mind from Doubt, Worry, Uncertainty and Fear

One night, about a month after we discovered our financial fortune was at risk and possibly all gone, I woke up in the middle of the night in a cold sweat. I couldn't get back to sleep; I kept thinking about the magnitude of our potential loss and berating myself for agreeing to put most of our money into this one investment. *How could I be so stupid? How could I let this happen?* I was paralyzed, stuck in the cycle of negative thinking.

As I raked myself over the coals, I would see the moment I signed the documents that set us on this course, in vivid detail. Then I would take a step further and remind myself of what I *could have* done with the money instead. I would beat myself up for blindly trusting the people who managed our money, even though they were our friends and it made perfect sense to trust them. Finally, when I was so riled up there was no hope of getting back to sleep, the fear would set in: fear of the unknown. *Crisis: A stage in a sequence of events at which the trend of all future events, especially for better or worse, is determined.*

It's the easiest thing in the world to revisit something negative that happened to us. It can be helpful to reflect on the event in order to find a solution or learn from the experience, but so often we slip back into obsessive thoughts: judgment and blame of ourselves and others. This negative thinking fuels and amplifies the anger, stress and anxiety we feel about the event and toward the other people involved.

As our mind continues to relive the event, the body believes it, experiencing all of the harmful negative emotions and stress as if the event were happening all over again. This affects every cell in the body, and our spirit. Staying on this path for any length of time has an impact on our health, and emotional and spiritual well-being, in the most profound and negative ways.

When we allow ourselves to get sucked in and focus all our energy on the things we (often) don't control, we become paralyzed. Yet as easy as it is to slide down this slippery slope, there is a simple way to counter this vicious cycle and regain control to take decisive action. In this chapter, I'll share my process for releasing the doubt, worries, uncertainty and fear that may keep *you* up at night.

YOUR OWN WORST ENEMY

My good friend Chris played professional golf for some time. Although his swing mechanics were great, he found it difficult to compete at the highest levels because he couldn't perform well consistently. Chris hired a coach to help him get to the heart of the problem.

His first session was on the golf course. His coach asked him after each swing to verbalize his thoughts, which she wrote down in a notebook. As he relayed his thoughts to her, he realized that, after each shot, he was under attack from his own mind. After a good shot, his mind would race with thoughts like, "You could have done better," or "Why couldn't you hit the same shot in the tournament?" After a bad shot, he would berate himself with bad names and verbal punishment unlike anything he had experienced from another person.

After six holes, she showed him pages and pages of negative self-talk. She said, "Enough! Stop talking to yourself that way. You will never be successful—not in golf or any other thing—until you stop doing this to yourself. You can't hate you! Until you get over this, I can do nothing to help your game. You've got to stop being your own worst enemy."

> *You've got to stop being*
> *your own worst enemy.*

Chris realized that his habit of punishing himself after bad shots was keeping him from a successful career as a professional golfer. Though he later retired from the sport, the experience he had on the course that day stayed with him for many years to come. It enabled him to silence his negative self-talk and become a successful entrepreneur in a field he genuinely loves.

Imagine the psychological impact on someone who is subjected to constant negative criticism from someone she loves and trusts. How would that name-calling, beration and admonishment affect her self-confidence and her desire to move forward in life, to seek answers and ask for help, to take a chance, to imagine a brighter future?

Now realize that, when you allow yourself to have these self-blaming, negative conversations in your head, *you* are that person. You are the person *you love and trust,* causing harm to yourself with relentless negative self-talk.

Like Chris, we're all in danger of falling prey to the hateful little person who sometimes lives inside of us. We expect a lot of ourselves, often more than those around us do. This is true in everyday life, but it is compounded in crisis, which is why it is paramount that we learn to control it. After all, getting through whatever situation has guided you to read this book is not about making more putts or hitting better shots. It's about your ability to thrive despite difficult times. *It's about your future.*

STEP ONE: THE "EVERYTHING" LIST

Before you can release the stuff that prevents you from moving on from a crisis, you have to name it—all of it. The first part of this powerful and effective exercise is to list all of the fears, worries and uncertainties that cross your mind on any given day. Write down everything—from the seemingly benign passing thoughts to the terrible fears that stop you in your tracks.

There are several benefits to making your own "Everything" list. First and foremost, you become aware of the scope of your concern. Sometimes we let worries overtake us without even realizing we're doing it. If you haven't named it, you can't release it!

Another benefit is the peace of mind the act of writing down your thoughts and concerns on paper provides. To know that the thoughts, emotions and worries that have been racing around in your mind are recorded, never to be lost or forgotten, is beneficial. Your mind doesn't have to hold on to them so tightly, nor does your mind have to repeat the same thoughts, emotions and worries over and over again to ensure that you *don't* forget. In this way, creating your "Everything" list has a similar benefit to writing a to-do list when you're overwhelmed—it calms the mind.

The list also legitimizes everything you're going through. The simple act of writing things down makes our thoughts,

> *If you haven't named it, you can't release it!*

emotions and worries real. It's all right there, in black and white. You're not crazy, or silly, or hysterical or overwrought; what you think and feel about the crisis is not up for debate.

Do you see now why it's so important to list everything?

After we lost the bulk of our fortune, the start of my "Everything" list looked something like this:

1. *I'm worried my money is all gone.*
2. *I'm afraid we will lose our homes.*
3. *I'm not sure I'll be able to find a job that pays well and would be enjoyable.*
4. *I'm afraid of losing the lifestyle and freedom and flexibility the money offered.*
5. *I'm upset, bitter, and angry at the people I trusted.*
6. *I'm upset and disappointed in myself for allowing this to happen....*

Creating your "Everything" list is the first step to releasing your worries, uncertainty and fear. It's your chance to purge all of it and get a sense of what you've been dealing with during your time of crisis.

STEP TWO: TAKE CONTROL

Having completed your "Everything" list, you are now ready to identify and separate the things you have control over versus the things you don't. This allows you to focus your energy on the things you do have control over, rather than deplete your energy focusing on things you *can't* control. This is where you will start to realize the powerful simplicity of this exercise. You will begin to regain your sense of control over the situation—beginning with your own reaction to it.

Look at every item on your list separately and ask yourself the following questions:

- Is this something I have control of?
- Can I put myself in a position of control, from which I can influence or change the outcome? Or at the very least, do I have the ability to take action?

Based on the first part of the "Everything" list I shared above, here is a sampling of my thought process about each item and what I wrote down as a result:

1. *It could drive me crazy to constantly think about the fact that my money is gone. It already happened, and worrying about the past doesn't serve any purpose. I can't control the fact that my money is gone, but I can control whatever money I have left.*

   Below Item 1, I wrote: "I can put myself in a position of controlling whatever money I have left."

2. *The fear of losing our homes is a reality I need to face, since we have no income coming in right now. I could wait and find out what monies we will recoup, if any, which means I would be using whatever precious money we have left to support the cost of operating two large homes. What we do have control over is deciding which home we want to keep. Then, once we decide, we can sell the other.*

   Below Item 2, I wrote: "I control and decide which home we wish to keep."

3. *I realize I need to find a job quickly to earn income. I hope I can find one that pays well and is enjoyable, but I don't have control over what the job will be, or when it will become available. I've been out of the workforce for some time, and I'm no longer plugged in to what is happening or what types of position may be available. But I do have a number of contacts who do have this knowledge and could possibly help me.*

   Below Item 3, I wrote: "I control all the tasks that will help me find a good job."

4. *As much as I enjoy the lifestyle, freedom and flexibility an abundance of money provided, I realize that I could still enjoy my life with less money. I could still enjoy freedom and flexibility if I chose to make it so. I could look for work opportunities that would be purposeful, enjoyable and offer a degree of freedom and flexibility.*

Below Item 4, I wrote: "I can control and adopt a positive attitude and seek work opportunities that will provide some degree of freedom and flexibility."

5. *As much as I am upset and angry with the people I trusted to manage our money, I also feel sorry for them. This situation is affecting their lives, families and employees as well. I realize that holding on to resentment and anger will serve no purpose in helping me to move forward and deal with the challenges I now face.*

    Below Item 5, I wrote: "I control where I direct my attention and energy. I can choose to focus on improving our *present situation*."

6. *And, as much as I am upset at myself, I know it will only harm me in the long run, so I won't allow myself to dwell on this very long. I need to use every ounce of energy toward improving our present situation.*

    Below Item 6, I wrote: "I have confidence in myself, and I will seek ways and opportunities to lead us out of this situation as quickly as possible. I will also learn and grow from this situation."

My "Everything" list could be much longer. It could have included a whole slew of "should've and could've" statements. If you need to put these down on your list, go ahead. It will help you to see every thought, emotion and worry that is causing you stress and preventing you from moving forward.

I didn't add these items to my list because all the "should've and could've" was in the past, and I knew that I couldn't affect, change or influence the past.

No amount of blaming yourself, or wondering if you could have handled a situation better or seen it coming, will change the fact that you are in crisis. There is nothing you can do about the past except learn from it, or seek a solution rooted in that lesson. Dwelling on the "should've and could've" will paralyze you, and you will get stuck.

If I had chosen to list all the things I "should've and could've" done to avoid my investment losses, under each one of those items, I'd simply have written: "No control on this one." The beauty of this exercise is, no matter whether you note the ways you have control over something or the fact that you have no control whatsoever, you can let go and move on. Realizing you have control and can make positive change

You do, however, have control over today.

enables you to let go of the worry that is based on feeling out of control. Likewise, realizing you have no control over a situation allows you to let go of the worry, because what difference will your worry make in the outcome anyway? The release is accomplished in shifting your focus and energy elsewhere—toward the positive change you *do* have control over. This is an essential step in moving forward.

. . .

Releasing negative thoughts, emotions and worries is a skill—a skill that requires practice. We are not born with this ability; it is not a gift, or a character trait that only some possess.

After I was demoted at work, I was stuck and paralyzed by the event for months. But years later, when we lost our fortune, I was able to shake off the negative self-talk quickly and move forward—*because* I had practiced this principle. Imagine that! Getting demoted is nothing compared to losing a ton of money, and yet I was able to move through the loss-of-fortune crisis easily.

You can't be successful if you hate yourself, and you can't get over this crisis if you don't stop the negative thinking that's keeping you up at night. You have no control over yesterday. You do, however, have control over today. Choose to put all of your energy and focus on the things you can change, influence and control, and let go of your concern over the things you cannot change, or have no control over.

1. What is your biggest fear about this issue?

2. What are your immediate concerns?

3. What are you afraid will happen as a result of this crisis?

4. What are your worries about how others will perceive your involvement in this?

5. What are your concerns about how your loved ones will handle this? Your boss, employees, colleagues? Your friends?

6. How could this situation change the way you view yourself? Your self-worth? Your ability to take action in the future?

7. What are your regrets, the things you said or did that you wish you could take back or do over?

8. How do you feel about this issue right now? How has it made an impact on your life?

9. What situation or event causes you to stir up negative self-talk?

10. Is this something you have control over?

11. Can you put yourself in a position of control, from which you can influence or change the outcome? Or at the very least, do you have the ability to take action?

Note: I created a free workbook for you, so that you can answer these and other questions and track your progress in one place. You'll also find helpful exercises. To download your free copy of *The Shatterproof Workbook*, go to shatterproofbook.com/resources.

Chapter 7

The Fifth Coping Principle: Create Your Future Circumstances Through Action

Before we dig into this next Shatterproof Coping Principle, I'd like you to take a moment to appreciate all that you've already accomplished, simply by reading this book and doing the corresponding exercises. First, you allowed yourself to become aware of and acknowledge the problem or crisis. You acknowledged that we reap what we sow, and that our thoughts, words and actions create our future circumstances. Then you accepted that you were in crisis and embraced the growth potential and transformative power that crisis can provide. Next, you gained control of the uncontrollable by exploring the worst-case scenarios, potential outcomes you had previously been afraid to consider. Then, through a simple written exercise, you released that which you could not control.

Though you may not feel the impact yet, you have done a lot of hard work! I hope that in doing this work, your mind has begun to shift away from fear and doubt. You may not yet *feel* calm or confident, but perhaps at least you can see that as a possibility for you.

It's as if, when you started becoming Shatterproof, you were in a broken-down car, out of gas and lost in a foreign land with no clue how to get home. Now that you've worked the first four Shatterproof Coping Principles, you've got the tools and parts to fix your car, you have a map and you're ready to take action. Soon enough, you'll find your way home.

Now that you've faced the worst-case scenario, learned how to control the "uncontrollable" and completed the process of releasing your fears, you are ready to take action on the aspects of your situation that you *can* control. This is the most crucial step by far on the path to regaining your confidence and getting your momentum back.

The very thing you are most afraid of, that thing that you fear will turn your world upside down and has you believing that from now on your world can only be doom and gloom— it doesn't have to ruin your life. Although you will experience

> *Baby steps are not only acceptable, they are pivotal.*

some change and you may never have your life back exactly the way it was, your life can become better and more enriching *because of that change*—if you choose to make it so. It's your choice. You are in control, and creating a brighter future begins with taking action on the things you can control. And it all starts with one baby step.

As you read through this chapter and complete the exercises, it's important to remember that you don't have to make giant leaps or sweeping changes. Baby steps are not only acceptable, they are pivotal. Baby steps create forward motion—once you're moving, you are on a path to create your future, one that is better than the situation you find yourself in today.

Taking baby steps can get you to the future you desire quickly because every step moves you forward, and, as you move forward, your progress has a ripple effect, creating positive outcomes and building your confidence much faster than one would imagine. Baby steps add up!

Remember my friend Mel's story in Chapter Five? After he imagined the worst-case scenario, he developed an action plan and then set action steps in motion that would ultimately create a *different* outcome. After Mel had his wake-up call in the hallway of the rehab center, he set goals for where he wanted to be by a certain time. His main goal was to be able to walk on his own to escort his girlfriend to the prom.

"I started enjoying going to physio and accomplishing something on a day-to-day basis. I didn't have to achieve something by leaps and bounds; I just focused on the small steps," Mel told me one afternoon. "I knew it was going to take time and that I had to be patient with the way the process would transpire. It was not a quick fix!"

Mel knew that he would not reach his goal overnight, but by taking steps each day he created a great deal of momentum, and for the first time since his accident he felt hope and renewed confidence. So what if there wasn't a silver-bullet solution? Every sensation, every tiny movement, every brief moment of being able to support his body weight was a win for Mel.

All of the baby steps added up to the vision Mel had for his future—to walk again. "I still remember the joy I had in taking my first steps. It was just absolute happiness and elation!"

By setting goals and taking baby steps toward those goals, Mel avoided his worst-case outcome and created his future. It really is that simple—you've already set the stage and done most of the hard work. Now it's time to take action and create *your* future.

HEALING IS AN ACTION WORD

When we view a crisis as the result of a personal failure or setback, we often tend to doubt our ability to recover from it, much less get our lives back on track. In my work helping people become Shatterproof, I've often been told, "I got myself into this mess; why should I believe I can get myself out of it?" This attitude causes them to sit day after day, passively observing, as things continue to fall apart and crumble before their very eyes.

Inaction can also be due to feeling physically taxed. Our bodies have real reactions to crisis—fatigue, loss of desire, inability to sleep and other symptoms that diminish our capacity to accomplish things. Ironically, *because* we are often depleted emotionally and physically during a crisis, the need to act is even more important. This is because we have to use whatever precious energy we have to be productive. We only have so much focus, energy and emotion to spend during a crisis and we must spend it on the things that will help us get to the other side of the crisis as quickly as possible.

Action in the face of crisis takes courage and intestinal fortitude. We may feel as if we just want to sit back and lick our wounds, or we may feel that the fight has taken too great a toll on us (mind, body and soul), and we need time to rest and heal. The problem with this is, you cannot undo the bomb that has blown up—there is a real aftermath that needs our attention. President John F. Kennedy perhaps said it best when he stated: "There are risks to action. But they are far less than the long-range risks of comfortable inaction."

It is human nature to come up with a host of reasons why "resting" (aka doing nothing) is the best way to heal from crisis. We're excellent at deferring action in other areas that need attention—such as a diet or exercise program, continuing education, the need for therapy, budget cuts or a frank talk with a loved one.

We can, in most cases, find perfectly logical reasons to postpone action based on what life is handing us at this very moment. We might say, "I was invited to dinner, so I'll start my diet tomorrow." Or, "I need to go back to school to be eligible for that promotion, but I'm so busy right now, I can't handle one more thing." Or, "I don't feel well. I'll exercise this weekend." On and on it goes as we pile on justifications for our avoidance.

It is in the moments when we feel as if we are too tired and beat up to keep going, and we just need a break to recharge our batteries, that taking action becomes critically important. It is paramount that you do not give in to the perfectly logical reasons that support your desire to give up. It is in these moments that your very future will be decided.

Healing is not a passive word. Healing is an action word. To heal, we must put one foot in front of the other and continue on, regardless of pain, anguish, exhaustion, sadness or depression.

One of the key things that we must train ourselves to do in crisis is look forward only. There will be time to look back; there will be time to contemplate the lessons and the meanings and to dig for those morsels of truth and good that will inevitably come. The time to do this is not, however, when you are still in the midst of a crisis. When you are in a crisis, the emotional currency you have must be spent focusing on the things that you can control and act on now—tasks, choices and tools that will help you focus on your future as opposed to the past and on accomplishing things that will leave your crisis in your rearview mirror.

TAKING CONTROL

To begin to take control of our situation, we first must go back to the previous chapter, in which we shifted our attention and energy toward identifying things we could control and releasing the things we could not control.

This Coping Principle is all about moving forward and creating motion. You achieve this by taking action on the things you can and do control. But before you take action, it's necessary to plan, so that the actions you take not only are impactful, but help you create a sustainable momentum.

Often, during a crisis, the situation can seem so stressful, enormous and overwhelming that you have no idea where to start. That's why it's so important to take baby steps, as Mel did, as I did when we lost the money, and as I did before that, when I was demoted.

Mel's baby steps, day in and day out, were small, measurable goals that he could take away as small victories each day. Momentum kept building, and after some time, he was finally able to take his "first walking step." When we look for quick fixes and silver bullets, we skip the baby steps; the big leaps are not sustainable. Mel couldn't skip any of the baby steps before he could get to that first walking step. He was building the foundation to support his body, making progress in tiny increments which added up over time and eventually enabled him to take his first actual step. Everything he did built strength and skill toward the goal, toward his vision. No results or achievements will ever happen without motion or baby steps.

When I was demoted and went from receiving the "produce or you're gone" ultimatum to ending up with the "Salesman of the Year" award, everything started with baby steps. I started by scheduling appointments with unqualified prospects and went to meet them face to face. I didn't have much success at the beginning. But I was in motion. I was playing on the court, in the game again, and this motion generated some level of energy and excitement. I was engaged.

I started feeling a little better about myself, a little more confident. My qualifying techniques and instincts started to resurface again, which resulted in my becoming more focused and disciplined. This eventually led to my improvement in qualifying clients and spending time with good prospects, which resulted in winning some small deals.

There's nothing like getting a taste of success, however small. You can't help but start feeling a whole lot better about yourself again. With every little success, my momentum increased. I also used fear to drive me in a positive way because, as I explained before, I never wanted to feel or experience that negative "space" again. I could easily and vividly recall how that felt, and there was no way in the world I wanted to go back. So I used this fear to drive, focus and motivate myself to continually move ahead; I was never satisfied where I was with each deal and success I reached. The more deals I got, the more I wanted and the more driven I became. My momentum and success increased because I was in motion. I wasn't standing still anymore. I was no longer paralyzed or stuck. I wasn't dwelling on the past, being a victim, assigning blame, or being helpless and hopeless anymore.

None of those things are possible when you're in *moving-forward motion*. And it all begins by taking baby steps!

To develop and plan your action list, begin with the list that you already compiled from "the things you can control." Under each of these, list the task, activity and action that need to take place, if appropriate. Here's a small sample of what my list looked like:

1. GET CONTROL OF REMAINING INVESTMENT		
ACTIVITY/TASK	**ACTION**	**WHEN**
Gather financial inv. acct. & statements	Pull paper files & electronic statements	By date
Decide which ones need to be moved, transferred or liquidated	Provide the necessary written instructions & direction to fund holder	By date
Once all investment sources are in my control, place in conservative investment option	Review & research conservative investment options	By date

2. DECIDE WHICH HOME TO KEEP

ACTIVITY/TASK	ACTION	WHEN
List pros & cons for each home	Summarize operating exp. of each home. Consider all factors, including location, climate, excitement, mental comfort, etc.	By date
Select real estate agent and list home	Interview 2-3 top real estate agents	By date
Prepare & stage home for sale	Get selected real estate agent to make recommendation & take action	By date

3. EXPLORE JOB MARKET OPPORTUNITIES

ACTIVITY/TASK	ACTION	WHEN
Establish contact with past colleagues & friends and seek their help	Compile contact list and contact everyone on that list	By date
Establish contact with potential employment placement agencies	Do research on the Internet to qualify which agencies would be the best fit	By date
Update résumé	Do research on the latest tips on preparing a great résumé	By date
Get plugged in to current trends	Do research and identify industry trends. Use the Internet, magazine, newsprint…	Daily

You'll notice that I didn't include items four to eight from my previous list. These items deal mainly with the attitude that I choose to adopt, so I'm aware of these and will catch myself when my mind starts drifting on the wrong path. But they're not something I'll list on the action plan.

The list is just to get you thinking about your own list; you can create yours any way you like.

Planning and preparing the action list in itself is therapeutic and empowering. This list, and acting on this list on a daily basis, saved me when I was going through my financial crisis. Building the list and acting on it gave me energy, satisfaction and confidence and brought a sense of control back into my life. I was in motion. And accomplishing something productive on a *daily basis* propelled me in a *sustainable forward motion*. We started taking action on getting our other investments under our control.

Once we agreed on which house to sell, the actions we took to prepare and stage the house for sale forced us to think ahead and take further action. Every little thing we accomplished brought satisfaction, pride and confidence. When someone came to see the house, we were excited and filled with hope that we would sell it. And within a few months, we got a great offer.

It's not that I didn't sometimes think about our loss of money or feel sad during this period. It's just that I caught myself, I was aware and I didn't permit myself to dwell on the negative; when that happened, I refocused my attention and shifted my mind back to the things I could control. And frankly, with all the activities that went on between selling the house, getting control of our other investments and reengaging with colleagues and friends to talk about potential work opportunities, I became excited again—I felt alive again! All this activity created new hope and excitement for me.

When you're doing all this, you find yourself thinking less and less of the past and are much more focused on the future and anticipation of what that future will bring. That's really powerful. And what I'm describing briefly here is the reason why losing a financial fortune didn't take me down, why I was able to overcome this challenge a lot less bruised and in a lot less time than when I got demoted.

Once you start planning and developing your action list, you'll find it is also the ideal place to add your goals and vision. This is an ideal time to ask, "Where do I want to go? What do I want to do?"

This is your chance to start with a clean slate, a new beginning that may perhaps be a long-held dream you never before had the courage to act on. Perhaps now is a good time to start building toward that goal and dream. You may

> This is an opportunity for you
> to create your own future.

need to go through various stages to get there, but this is an opportunity for you to start planning and putting your wheels in motion to go after that dream. This is an opportunity for you to create your own future. But realize: Your goals and vision will only be attained when you create motion by performing daily activities that are aligned toward reaching them.

Mel chose to create his own future. He not only wanted to walk again, he also had a powerful vision of walking into the prom with his girlfriend on his arm. Mel said, "The one thing I did learn is that when you're honest with yourself and you put that vision out there, you don't have to repeat it a whole bunch of times to yourself because it just becomes part of you. It's not something that you have to continually convince yourself that that's what the vision is… you simply know what you have to do every day."

> *A vision that you create and*
> *own will pull you along.*

A vision that you create and own will naturally and automatically drive you, fuel you and pull you along.

Once your action list is built and complete, wherever you start, make sure that you select the baby steps that you are one hundred percent sure you will be able to accomplish in a very short period of time. This is so important because you've been bruised and perhaps deeply affected by your challenge and crisis, and you need to build strength and confidence and gain back control. You accomplish this by completing something, by achieving some kind of result. It does not have to be big or significant. You just need to get going doing something.

After you complete your first baby step, you will immediately gain confidence and feel a sense of accomplishment, control and power, which, until now, you thought had been taken away from you. By continuing down this path in a sustainable way, by continually doing baby steps and breaking every project, every objective, every goal into small, bite-sized pieces, remaining in perpetual motion, you will achieve results! It's impossible not to!

. . .

Action will not happen automatically. Confidence and a sense of control will not somehow magically appear one day, and in all likelihood, you will not feel any better about starting tomorrow than you do today. So take the step—one small baby step. Create your list. Make the call. Fill out the forms. Ask for help. Do whatever you can do *today* to begin to move out of this crisis. And tomorrow, do it again.

Remember, that broken-down car of yours now has a little gas, enough to start the car and get you farther down the road. And unlike real-world cars, the more you drive this one, the faster you fill up that tank. Your action list in hand, with every baby step you take, with every task you complete, you are not

> *Do whatever you can do today to*
> *begin to move out of this crisis.*

only putting more gas in the tank, you are also equipping your car with a GPS system (your plan) that will give you focus and direction. With this GPS system, you will find your way out of your situation quickly. You now know where you're going and how you're going to get there—and you are equipped with a vehicle that will get you where you need to go.

You worked hard. You've got this. You can handle any and all challenges and make real progress toward reclaiming the contentment that is your birthright. You are *not* stuck in a broken-down car with no hope of getting where you want to go. You are driving, moving forward with tools, resources and a renewed sense of confidence that will help you arrive at your destination quickly, and without added stress. Roadblocks—who cares? Flat tire—you can handle it. Detour—no problem!

You've got this.

Now take the first step.

1. If you have not created your own Shatterproof Action List, do it now. If you completed the exercise in the previous chapter, you already have most of the work done.

2. Identify one baby step you can accomplish today and take action!

3. After you complete your first task, take note of how you feel. For some of you, this will be the first step you've taken since you started dealing with whatever stress, challenge or crisis inspired you to read this book. How does it feel to make progress, however tiny the step?

4. Now, choose another baby step and schedule time to complete it.

Note: I created a free workbook for you, so that you can answer these and other questions and track your progress in one place. You'll also find helpful exercises. To download your free copy of *The Shatterproof Workbook*, go to shatterproofbook.com/resources.

Chapter 8

The Sixth Coping Principle: Secure Serenity Through Gratitude

A grateful mind is a great mind which eventually attracts to itself great things.
Plato

Toward the end of Carol's life, she was too weak to feed herself. I would sit as close to her hospital bed as possible and spoon-feed her soup and pudding with her medication mixed in. It seemed like a simple task—fill the spoon, put it in her mouth, fill the spoon, put it in her mouth—but it took me a while to get the hang of it. I was too quick, and tried to shove one heaping spoonful after another into her mouth. Carol corrected me. "Slow down. Put smaller amounts on the spoon," she said.

The next time I fed her, I remembered her instructions. I tapped off the excess pudding before I placed the spoon in her mouth, and waited until she was finished to offer her another spoonful. "That's perfect," she said. "It's just the right amount of pudding and just the right pace." She kept complimenting me, and soon I felt better about my ability to care for her. She kept praising me, so much so that I eventually thought: *I'm the best spoon-feeder in the world!*

It may seem like a small victory, but it was everything to me. Before Carol's diagnosis, I just couldn't handle watching people suffer. Watching children or my wife in physical pain or discomfort made me weak in the knees. I couldn't clean wounds or change bandages. I almost fainted every time I received a shot or saw someone else getting injected with a needle. When Carol had routine elective surgery, she became nauseated from the anesthesia. Watching her throw up, I became faint. The nurse had to leave Carol's side to come and help me! I was *not* the person you wanted taking care of you when you were sick, no way.

Becoming a caregiver for my wife eliminated those weak tendencies. I changed bandages on her wounds, administered needles for blood thinning and rubbed her back when she vomited. I don't know how I did it, but I did. I never had to psych myself up to do it, either. It just happened, like flipping a switch. I was there for her, supporting her in any way necessary. And I never felt faint, or scared or nervous. In caring for Carol, I discovered a strength I never thought I would have.

One day, after I had mastered the art of spoon-feeding, Carol looked at me and said, "It's amazing, but I can't believe that even at this stage in our life, our love continues to grow." I nodded and smiled, because she was so, so right. Even after thirty years of devotion, this was a new level of intimacy for us. It was special, an experience not to fear or complain about, but to treasure. She reached for my hand and continued, "I can't believe that our love just grew to a whole new level. It's absolutely wonderful and beautiful that we can experience this together."

Many crises are steeped in loss, or the risk of loss—a home in jeopardy of foreclosure, a relationship dissolving, a beloved wife and mother slowly slipping away—and all that represents: loss of lifestyle, identity, community, whatever is tied, for you, to the person, thing or role you are at risk of losing. You feel your confidence, your sense of security and your sense of being in control are at risk, and that seems like a loss, too. And when you feel out of control and insecure, there is little hope of calm; there is mostly anxiety and chaos.

When Carol was diagnosed, I knew I was losing my wife, the woman I had loved since I was a boy of nineteen. But I was also losing my love, my joy, my best friend, my confidante, my companion, my biggest supporter and my biggest fan. It seemed like I was losing everything. Just... everything. It would have been easy—and "perfectly understandable"—to choose the path of self-destruction and put all of my thoughts and energy into the loss of my sweetheart. Instead, my focus became one of gratitude.

In the previous chapters, you have learned simple ways to tame your worry and gain confidence in dealing with a crisis, all of which will surely give you respite. And, the surest way not only to achieve serenity in the midst of crisis, but to secure it, is to practice gratitude—gratitude for *all things*.

In gratitude, we don't have the time or energy to project into the future or fret over the past. In gratitude, we don't have room for negative thoughts about our own choices or the actions of others. In gratitude, we are at ease, because we know that in every experience, "good" or "bad," there is opportunity—to learn, to grow, to appreciate and to understand.

THE SERENITY TRACK

Our natural reactions in a crisis are patterns we have become very accustomed to, even without thinking. We experience a setback or a loss and immediately focus on what was or will be lost. Our minds race with thoughts about how much we loved that which we've lost, how our lives will be different without it, and what we'll have to do to get it back or replace it. We push ourselves to the brink of insanity trying to undo, relive and replace the possessions, people, status, experiences and promises that slipped away.

For many people, this can be the first step that leads to depression, overwhelming anxiety, physical ailments or even worse. Remember, the body believes what the mind is thinking—so, when you revisit the loss over and over again, your body is experiencing the event as if it's really happening. In this way, one crisis leads to another, and another, until life seems cruel or unbearable.

Caught up in this loss cycle, we miss out on the opportunity that crisis can provide and instead sink further into anxiety and depression. It is gratitude that gets us back on track to serenity, and eventually happiness.

In his article, "Two New Studies Show the Power of Gratitude and Kindness,"[4] Dr. Michael Murray described a 2005 review article in *American Psychologist*: "Positive Psychology in Progress. Empirical Validation of Interventions," co-authored by Martin Seligman, PhD, former president of the American Psychology Association and a thought leader in the discipline of positive psychology. Of the article, Dr. Murray wrote, "Seligman described a study in which participants were randomly assigned to one of six therapeutic interventions designed to improve their overall quality of life. Of these six interventions, it was found that the most significant short-term effects came from a 'gratitude visit' in which participants wrote and delivered a letter of appreciation to someone in their life. This simple gesture caused a significant rise in happiness scores and a significant fall in depression scores, and the positive effects lasted up to one month after the visit."

This reminds me of the night we received the news that Carol had very little time left to live. It was several hours before they finally gave us a bed in the emergency room so that she could lie down. My mind raced with thoughts about the conversations we'd had with doctors. I kept thinking, *How can this be real? This is what happens to other people, not us.*

Carol said, "Lie down next to me, facing me. You can share my pillow." It was the first time we had been alone together since the crisis happened; I felt such a sense of closeness and intimacy! With her big, sparkling eyes Carol looked at me, smiled warmly and said, "We're so lucky! We're so lucky to have lived thirty years together, loving each other for *thirty years.* That is a lifetime that most people never get to experience."

Rather than dwell on the inevitable loss we would both experience in the near future, *that* was the conversation Carol chose to have that evening. Cuddled up close, we stayed up all night reminiscing about our life and all our beautiful moments together, grateful for each and every one. As I focused on the amazing experiences we had shared, my mind began to quiet.

In place of worry and fear, I saw the joy and the happiness we were so fortunate to have, and it instantly changed my entire outlook on the situation. We *were* so lucky, so very lucky. Right there in the emergency room, holding my terminally ill wife, that realization dried my tears and brought a smile to my face.

A SHIFT IN PERSPECTIVE

In my travels, I've seen firsthand that material possessions and financial status have very little to do with achieving and maintaining an overall sense of well-being. Those of us who have more than enough money often experience less joy, peace and happiness than those with far less. According to the *HealthDay Reporter* article by Jennifer Goodwin,[5] a Princeton University study determined Americans with an annual household income of at least $75,000 do not gain happiness in proportion to increases in income. That means, once they've reached the $75,000 threshold, money certainly does not buy happiness.

This is not to say that a life devoid of material possessions is somehow a greater calling than a life of abundance, but it is important to begin to understand why, so we do not fall into these same traps. Having, in and of itself, is not something we should seek to avoid. It is not the act of having that is the impetus for being unhappy. The problem is, we place too much value on material possessions while taking those possessions for granted at the same time.

Think back to something as simple as your last meal. Were you actively grateful for it? Most probably, like most of us, you did not give thanks. In our lives, we have a tendency to take the status quo for granted. We overlook how grateful we should be for those things that we do have, experience or become. In a crisis, as we focus on that thing or things that we lost, we can even begin to think more about what we don't have than what we do have.

Today's mainstream media—especially the advertising world—has made it a stated goal to influence consumers to believe that, without the products, services and ideas the advertisers are promoting, they simply can no longer be content with their lives. This is not an accident, it is not a byproduct; it is the goal, and a tendency we must keep in check in our own lives.

The act of embracing gratitude is not some "out there" concept reserved for mountaintop monks and religious zealots. It is a state of mind we must train ourselves to live in. It is not simply an activity, but rather a shift in how we see the world around us.

TAKING STOCK

As Carol's illness progressed, I took inventory. I thought about how blessed I was to have had thirty wonderful years with her, filled with so many memories, so many great moments—a lifetime of quality and unconditional love. I thought about our beautiful daughter and grandson, two angels in my life with whom to exchange love and support. My mind drifted to my loving parents, brothers, and sister and their families, and to my close friends and colleagues, all of whom I love and in turn surround me with love. I thought about my life's vision— to help people conquer any crisis and adversity, to become Shatterproof—and what a gift and honor it is to be called to this purpose. With the acknowledgment of each blessing, my heart filled with gratitude.

And perhaps the most profound gift of the experience: the lesson to live "full-out," to take advantage of each moment here and now, because we don't know when we'll be called to go through our own transition and leave this earth. Sure, I had understood that in theory. But to come face to face with death, to watch Carol reconcile this in her own mind and come to terms with it, that was profound. I got it. I truly got it. As I go through life without my beloved Carol, this gift, this lesson, stays with me and propels me forward. In fact, it is because of this gift that you are reading this book right now.

Living full-out is not about doing the crazy thing or embarking on risky adventures; it's about consciously connecting with yourself and all that surrounds you. It's about cultivating awareness about life and cherishing all that you have, all that you feel and all that you experience. When you live full-out, you feel connected to everyone you come in contact with and to the beauty of the environment. In gratitude, each moment can be sacred. How we direct the activity of the mind shapes our consciousness and enables us to heal ourselves and radiate joy to others we come into contact with. This is living *full-out*.

Taking a gratitude inventory of your life is an essential step in becoming Shatterproof, because it takes you out of the chaos of emotion, worry and stress and brings you back to the present moment so you can better deal with the crisis at hand. It gives you perspective. You start to see that life has been pretty good to you. And, in taking stock of all of your many blessings, you are better able to find joy in *all* things—even the painful stuff.

. . .

At the end of this chapter, you'll find an exercise to help you create your own list. You don't have to complete your gratitude inventory in one day or even one week. Just write down as much as you can and then come back to it as soon as you can. Add to it each time you feel lucky, blessed or fortunate. And refer to it often. Ground yourself in the truth of your experience and let gratitude lift you out of the noise and chaos of crisis to live fully in the present.

Your gratitude list will prove incredibly useful in helping you shift the way you think—it will enable you to move away from past loss and negative experiences, detach from all that has transpired and let go of regret.

In the last precious months with Carol, I created a gratitude list in my mind, adding to it every day. It was easy to build a gratitude inventory, because we had such an amazing life together. My list was largely centered on our family and us,

*Living in gratitude leaves little
room for anything else.*

because that was my focus at the time, and it was made up of a lot of memories. The day we met. Driving 180 miles to see her each weekend. Coming back together—for good—after a six-month separation. Our trips to the Rocky Mountains. All of the moments I confided in her. All of the moments we leaned on each other. All of the moments we celebrated our love.

Carol was living in gratitude up until her very last breath. I thought, *If she can look at our life together and be so thankful for the love we've had—a lifetime, she called it—how could I not look at what we had in the same way? How could I not be in a complete state of gratitude?*

When you review your list, you will find that you spend less time focusing on what you've lost, or might lose, and more time focusing on what you do have. How can you not look at

Gratitude is the path to faith.

all that you've witnessed, all that you've learned, all that you've been given, all that you've experienced, and not be in a complete state of gratitude?

And if you're in a complete state of gratitude, how can you be stuck in crisis mode? Living in gratitude leaves little room for anything else.

GRATITUDE IS A CHOICE

Gratitude is not something we experience passively. Gratitude is an action, a choice we make to focus on something other than the negative, self-defeating thoughts that can trap us in a chaotic loop of anxiety, depression and illness.

Gratitude is not a replacement for action or momentum and should not be considered as such. There is a reason that this step comes after the action component of this process. Do not mistake gratitude for something you will use to hide from the reality of a situation, or something that will give you permission to ignore the gravity of a crisis.

Gratitude is the path to faith, which we discuss in the next chapter. Through gratitude, we gain serenity about the situation we are experiencing and a belief in the eventual gift the experience will provide.

Remember the saying, "When a door closes, another one opens," or, "When a door closes, a window opens?" Being grateful allows you to separate from anxiety so that you can actually *see* the doors open to you, can see the light that is there even if those doors are open just a crack. In my own life, I have watched those around me spend time banging on the closed

> *Without gratitude, it will never be enough—it will never fill that void inside of you.*

door, trying to find a way to reopen it, and talking about how it never should have closed and how much they wish that it would open once again. They have missed the opportunity to move on and open the new and better doors they could have availed themselves of, if only they would turn their heads and look. How many of us are missing out on opportunities to grow a bigger box, to expand our knowledge and wisdom, because we are trapped in thoughts of all we have lost?

Life is full of opportunities, and that is one of the things that I am most grateful for. No matter what the economy is doing, no matter what happens on Wall Street, we as people have the opportunity to live extraordinary lives, filled with peace, hope and fulfillment. It is, however, a prerequisite that you learn to embrace a life filled with gratitude. Without gratitude, no matter how many things you have or don't have, no matter how wonderful your relationships, your health or whatever else, it will never be enough—it will never fill that void inside of you.

Not a day goes by that I do not feel grateful about every aspect of my life. I have and live an extraordinary life. I live every day in a state of gratitude. I choose and live it in awareness every day, and I'm thankful for all that I have in my life. I am grateful for all the little things, like the comfort of my bed and the home I am privileged to own; the clean water and clean air I'm exposed to; the beautiful sunsets I experience while I run on the beach, watching dolphins swim; the magical, beautiful nature I'm surrounded by... all these little miracles that surround me and that I connect with. The list is endless, and, throughout the day, as I experience different things, I remind myself how grateful I am to live in this world, here and now!

Here's another example of tapping into this conscious gratitude state at a moment's notice, as a reminder to live full-out in appreciation of the present moment: While golfing with my buddies in Florida, waiting on the tee-blocks, I often zone in on the natural beauty that surrounds me: the long shadows cast by palm trees; a gator head, slightly raised in the middle

*Joy is created by focusing on
the "little things" life offers.*

of the calm waters of the lake; small turtles, basking in the sun on rocks off the shoreline. I notice the big, white, puffy clouds in motion against the backdrop of the beautiful blue sky, the warm breeze that comes and goes, the white egret patiently and slowly walking the shore and waiting to lunge for its prey.

Noticing the beauty all around me, I'm conscious. I'm focused. I'm present. A feeling of joy and contentment instantly infuses my mind and body as I fall into a complete state of appreciation and gratitude. I am thankful for the life I have here and now.

All this happens in a matter of seconds, but the connection is profound. A short wave of bliss overtakes me, like a sudden light breeze. My golf game experience instantly expands into a much more joyous, delightful process than it would ever be if I were simply contemplating a missed putt or errant shot or worrying about my next drive from the tee! I'm totally present. New moments of pure joy are created, all focused on the "little things" life offers. How many of those are we missing each day?

Living in a state of gratitude each and every day is a mindset I chose to adopt. Gratitude awareness is very powerful. It's a way of life. When living in this mindset, you can't help but feel content, joyful and happy, because you are living in a state of abundance.

•　•　•

At the end of Carol's life, the drugs and pain medication made her confused at times, especially at night. I had to give her a pill between eleven p.m. and midnight, one that required she take it with food. She would become confused and not want to eat the pudding. But she trusted me completely.

I would say to her, "But you love this special pudding."

She would look at me with her big beautiful hazel eyes and in the sweetest, melodic voice, she would say, "I *do*?"

"Yes you do, sweetie," I would answer, and she'd open her mouth without hesitation so I could spoon-feed her the medicine.

And for her implicit trust, for her beautiful eyes, for her melodic voice and for those quiet moments in the middle of the night, spoon-feeding my wife, I am eternally grateful.

Taking inventory of life's many blessings allows us to detach from loss and let go, opening up space for something else to enter our lives. We may not see the new door opening for some time; we may not be ready. But it is through a regular

Gratitude is a higher way of living.

practice of gratitude that we allow the new open door to come into our lives at all. Gratitude allows us to welcome the endless possibilities that exist for us. Through remembering and honoring whom we are, and whom we once were, we find the courage to begin again.

In the serenity provided by living in gratitude, we are able to create new moments and new good and memorable experiences, even in the midst of crisis—an intimate moment in an emergency room, a new level of love in a spoonful of pudding.

Gratitude is a higher way of living. It is a paradigm shift that will bring you a comfort and peace nothing else can provide. Do not underestimate the value of it; do not cheapen it or try to defer it until after you get to a certain place or time in your life. We may believe that being Shatterproof is about becoming stronger. While that's true, it's much more about realizing we are truly blessed.

Taking a gratitude inventory isn't just a concept; it really works. It can make you feel better, calmer and more present almost instantly—and every time you read it. Your gratitude list will prove incredibly useful as you shift your thinking from a negative state to a more joyous, contented mindset. You can fill in the blanks in this book, or you can write in your own notebook or on your own tablet. No time like the present.

Write down everything you're grateful for: the big stuff, the little stuff, and everything in between. Think about your loved ones: the experiences you've had, the lessons you've learned, the privileges you've enjoyed. Think about your teachers, mentors, heroes and role models. Think about your surroundings, your comforts and the beauty you see day in and day out.

Here are a few questions to get you started:

1. **Whom do you love?** Make a list of all of the people you have had the privilege of knowing and loving in your life: family, friends, lovers, teachers, coaches and leaders.

2. **What have you learned?** Jot down all of the amazing educational experiences you've had, as well as the life lessons you've experienced firsthand and the wisdom passed down to you from others.

3. **Where is the magic?** Write down all of the amazing moments or experiences you've had that truly seemed magical, or miraculous or fated.

4. **How have you been blessed?** Make a list of all of the ways in which you are fortunate. Are you in good health? Have you achieved goals or dreams or both? Do you enjoy the comforts and safety of a nice home and community? Are you surrounded by natural beauty? Do you enjoy certain freedoms?

5. **What will you remember?** Jot down the moments that you feel lucky to have had: perhaps the day you met your spouse, or gave birth to a child or shared a special night with true friends. Maybe it's the sunset you'll never forget, or the conversation you had with a stranger, or a moment you felt truly proud of yourself.

Note: I created a free workbook for you, so that you can answer these and other questions and track your progress in one place. You'll also find helpful exercises. To download your free copy of *The Shatterproof Workbook*, go to shatterproofbook.com/resources.

Chapter 9

The Seventh Coping Principle: Gain Unsinkable Confidence Through Faith

The term "crisis of faith" is one commonly used in Western culture to describe an event or experience that causes one to question their beliefs. Whether we subscribe to a specific religion or none at all, we've all had experiences that *feel* the way a crisis of faith feels: like an intense (and often debilitating) doubt.

A crisis or unexpected event can shake your confidence and cause you to doubt yourself, your loved ones, your colleagues, authority figures and your friends. As you discovered earlier in the book, the climax of a crisis is when you reach the point where you have no idea what will happen next. This is when your fear of the unknown depletes your confidence. In this way, a crisis of faith is also a crisis of confidence.

So what exactly is confidence? The Webster Dictionary defines confidence as a feeling or consciousness of one's power. The feelings that come up when you're in crisis—fear, anxiety, loss of control, worry, anger, resentment—all of these chip away at your confidence, *your faith in your own power to weather any storm.*

When you allow yourself to dwell in the negative emotional state of fear and uncertainty, doubting yourself and feeling insecure about your own abilities to handle the situation, you will not only feel anxious and stressed out, you may also get stuck in this state. And as you know from reading the previous chapters, this paralysis seriously hampers your ability to achieve productive growth and goals.

When you're feeling confident, when you feel empowered—when you *have faith* in your own power—you can confront and get through *any* difficult situation you may face.

So how do you regain confidence when crisis has stripped it from you? How can you find that inner core of strength when all you want to do is stick your head in the sand and wait for the dust to settle? How can you make it through unexpected stresses and events if it seems you've lost the ability to tap into your own power?

The answer is simple: faith in a power greater than yourself.

Today in America, if you were to ask the question, "Do you believe in God?" the vast majority would answer "yes." (According to the Wikipedia article "Religion in the United States," a 2011 Gallup poll found that ninety-two percent of Americans said yes to that question.)

The majority of us believe in God or a higher power. With this in mind, I will proceed and mention "God" or "higher power" with the intention that you fill in the blank as to what God or higher power you connect with.

It's important that we take a moment to define "faith" for the purposes of this book. This is not a religious text; I am not promoting a particular religion or set of beliefs. I am not pointing to a particular deity, God, the universe, or otherwise.

Faith, as I define it here, is the belief that there is a higher being or power which allows us to have experiences in life that will help us become the people we were meant to become. Faith is also the understanding that there is a purpose in everything, and we are not simply subject to a random string of events.

Simply put, when you experience a crisis of faith or confidence in your own abilities to handle a situation, faith in a higher power will carry you through and renew your confidence. In fact, it is my belief that faith in a higher power will give you *unshakable* confidence, the final step in becoming Shatterproof.

We all know what it's like to doubt our abilities, our worth, our strength and our courage. As we explored the previous six Coping Principles and moved toward conquering whatever crisis brought you to this book, you may have felt some of that doubt ebb a bit. You may be feeling some of your confidence

> *Faith in a higher power will give you unshakable confidence.*

return. Or, you may still be looking at confidence in your rearview mirror, wondering what happened to your ability to move forward with your head held high.

As fragile as you may feel during this time, know that this is your time for self-awareness, which will lead you to self-discovery. Regardless of where you are in the journey, know that you will regain your confidence—in fact, I wouldn't be surprised if you came out of this crisis even more confident, with a renewed faith in your own abilities and a stronger sense of your own power than you had before crisis knocked you for a loop.

THE POWER OF FAITH

Think about it—you've already taken a "leap of faith." Twice! First, you picked up this book and decided to read it, putting your faith in me, and in your ability to follow the Seven Coping Principles. Then, in the Second Coping Principle, you embraced and accepted crisis, which in its own way was also a leap of faith—and in this case, it *was* a faith in your higher power, the unseen force that has the ability to see the bigger picture and steer us in the right direction. In that act of acceptance, you experienced faith. And, if nothing else, you followed your intuition.

Our lives are filled with up and down cycles. When we're on a high, everything seems to go our way, and we experience the greatest joys and moments of happiness. In this state, life flows naturally in a perfect rhythm and success seems easily attainable. When the cycle changes, suddenly everything seems to be difficult and challenging. We feel vulnerable and start second-guessing our decisions and doubting our abilities. We become stagnant.

In these down periods, you may ask yourself, *What have I done wrong?* Yet without experiencing these dark periods, you would not grow, you would not evolve. Each difficult experience delivers a special message to you, so you mustn't give way to despair, bitterness or insecurity. As fragile as you may feel, know that this is your time of self-discovery, and that it will ultimately prove to be a greater blessing than those blessings you experienced in the high periods of your life, when all was well.

When we are caught up in the climax of a crisis, fearing the unknown, faith is often the *only* pillar that we have to

123

hold on to. The enormous strength that this pillar can offer is immeasurable and often beyond human comprehension. Faith in a higher power will give you the courage to move forward, to take that one step, and give you purpose so you do not fold, you do not crumble. When you are drowning in fear and all seems bleak, lost and hopeless, faith is your lifeboat.

You will never know how strong you are until you are faced with something for which a positive outcome seems impossible. It is in these climactic moments of crisis that we connect to a higher power—how many times have you heard a story of someone praying to God for help, or tapping into intuition to successfully navigate a dangerous and seemingly hopeless scenario?

Perhaps the most powerful story I have heard about harnessing the immense strength and protection provided through connection to a higher power is my friend Francine's story. In her absolute darkest and most frightening moment, in the midst of an unimaginable crisis, she let faith see her through.

"The night before the event happened, I had a very bad dream. In my dream, someone was trying to get into my house, and I was trying as fast as I could to close all the windows and lock all the doors. I woke up with the feeling that something really bad was going to happen and that it had to do with me, and that it was something that I would not be able to stop. I cannot tell you how much I tried to wiggle out of my upcoming trip and come up with any way possible or a good enough excuse not to go, because I felt *so strongly* that something was about to happen and that I could not stop it,"

Francine told me one day, when I asked her to share her story with readers.

"I remember being on the airplane and asking myself, *Do you really trust yourself to be all that you can be and really fully show up if something very dramatic happens? Do you know for certain that you will rise above it?* And I thought, *Yeah, I think so!*

"I arrived at my hotel and settled in my room. As our company had people traveling extensively, including around the world, we had executive privileges at the hotel. Having worked in a hotel setting before, I was very aware and knowledgeable of the various types of procedures and protocol that different hotel services offered. Settling in my room, I received a knock on the door, and this wasn't unusual, since the staff at the hotel were likely simply verifying if I needed anything, if the room was okay, if I needed more towels. I was not at all expecting to see anyone else other than a hotel staff person at the door. I asked who it was and the person replied, 'Hotel staff,' and I opened the door. And there he was. I knew instantly what was about to take place," Francine continued.

What happened next was an atrocious and hideous act. Francine was raped in her hotel room.

"What allowed me to cope and not lose it during this episode of sheer brutality at the hands of this guy was that I immediately felt a direct connection to God. I truly felt and heard the words, 'You're going to be okay,' and felt calmness in the midst of total chaos. It was as if there was someone there guiding me and assuring me that I *was* going to be okay; that this man could touch my body but *not* my soul," Francine explained.

"I knew I needed to remain levelheaded about what was happening, almost like overpowering him with my thoughts so that he could not hurt me, or perhaps he would choose not to do certain things. There was that unbelievable connection and feeling that I was being protected, and I felt surrounded by an aura of love in addition to this sense of protection that allowed me to stay calm in the midst of the violence that was

> *Our reactions, or lack thereof, become defining moments in our lives.*

happening to me. It allowed me to make very objective decisions immediately after the attack as opposed to falling apart."

We aren't always one hundred percent responsible for some of the circumstances in our lives, and sometimes, like Francine, we are not responsible at all, but we are always one hundred percent responsible for how we choose to react to them—that is our choice! Our reactions, or lack thereof, become defining moments in our lives.

The first thing Francine did after the attack was call the hotel staff so that she could get to the hospital and get herself checked. And when the sexual assault squad showed up, she stunned them by asking if she could get in a police car with them and start scouring the streets looking for the man who had just attacked her. They were amazed that someone who had just gone through something so traumatic would choose to focus on what she could do to make a difference.

"I knew I could not undo what was done to me, but my first thought was, *I'll be damned if I don't do something that could get this guy off the street.* Because I didn't want what had just happened to me to happen to another woman, and I had a responsibility to help get this guy off the street," Francine said.

Francine and the police scoured the city and surrounding areas for a few hours, and then went to the police station and looked at photos of thousands of convicted rapists and child molesters they had in their database. Unfortunately, her attacker was not found in their database. They then worked with the staff composite artist to create an image of the perpetrator to distribute to all the establishments and hotels in the area.

"I felt really empowered to make those choices, because to me, it was part of the healing process. I became instrumental in catching this guy. I even went undercover for a while. And I went to the police station many times when there was a lineup for me to identify until one day, we finally caught him," Francine explained.

"During the trial, it became the first time in court that they admitted DNA as evidence in rape cases in Canada. I was making history and changing things so that it would make it easier for people after me. I had a very good prosecutor and I had an amazing team all around me. I think that they were all motivated to go beyond their line of duty because they were so inspired by the way I reacted.

"I refused to be the victim and I was taking a very active part in helping them the best way I could and being *right there* with them. They really wanted to do good and catch this guy—to change the laws and do whatever was necessary to make this traumatic event not go in vain for any of us involved."

There is a reason that adversity, crises and setbacks often become the defining moments of our lives. It is through these experiences that we become much more aware of our strengths and our abilities. We don't grow by dodging bullets or trying to avoid reality, or by sitting idle on the sidelines. We grow because we accept and embrace change, because we acknowledge that there is a greater force at work offering us opportunities *for* growth, and because we go fearlessly into the unknown with faith as our guide and protector.

Change is inevitable. It's going to happen. Progress and growth, on the other hand, are totally optional.

It is in these difficult, teachable moments that we begin to see how we react to crisis, change and stress, and how we get to know who we are and what we are capable of doing.

When Francine finished her triumphant story of courage and faith, she said, "It was interesting that when I was on the plane, wondering if I could handle whatever bad thing was about to happen, I thought, *I think so.* After the event happened, I thought, *I know so.* I knew for sure."

When, like Francine, you manage to get through such a situation, your confidence and your belief, your faith in the power within you will become immeasurable. Realize that this power was always there—you simply didn't know of its existence until you were forced to use it. Once you become aware of the magnitude of your own power, you can harness it, not only to help you overcome difficulties, but also to propel you to create and obtain all the goals and dreams you wish for! Leverage it as your fuel of creation. Ask yourself: "What is my true potential? What's inside me waiting to come out?"

LETTING GO OF EMOTIONAL BAGGAGE

How many of us have been affected by past events? How many of us hold on to this negative situation, unable to let go? Often, the event has caused us to hold a great deal of resentment toward the person who caused us pain and suffering.

Right now, think of something toward which you feel resentment. Ask yourself, "What good does it do me to remember this event?"

Going back and remembering this event, observe all the negative emotions that you instantly feel. (Remember, the body believes what the mind thinks.) Observe how you are effectively fueling anger, hatred and resentment by holding on

> *"How did all this resentment serve me throughout my life?"*

to and revisiting this situation. And, while observing, keep asking yourself, "How can holding on to this resentment possibly serve me? How does this make my life better and happier? What good does it do for me to hold on to the negative emotions I feel toward this person?"

Now I want you to imagine yourself being informed that you have but a few months to live. There are no solutions to get you out of this prognosis. You've had time to digest that news and you're now reflecting on your life. While doing this, you become aware of all the time and energy you spent resenting certain people, and the negative emotional impact that had on you. And you ask yourself, "How did all this resentment serve me throughout my life?"

Sitting in the car outside the doctor's office, after he gave us the news that they had found a mass via CAT scan and needed to explore further via MRI, Carol's first words to me were, "You know where this came from?" She knew the source: her anger and resentment toward our financial crisis and the people who caused it. In her mind, this was confirmed when the ER doctor said, "A tumor that size in your brain would likely take seven to eight years to grow." It was seven years to the month since we had lost our fortune. Were the negative emotions she had harbored the entire cause of her cancer? Probably not. But did holding on to all of that resentment end her life prematurely? Without a doubt. Did Carol believe that this and other resentments she held were the cause of her cancer? Absolutely!

In addition to using and harnessing faith as your guiding and protective light, you can deploy your connection to your higher power to help you detach and let go of any negative emotions or resentment that have remained locked inside of you—like breaking a spell. Surrendering all the toxic, negative emotions entrenched in your deepest core will give you an overwhelming sense of freedom and liberation that could seem unimaginable in the midst of your crisis.

When Carol was able to let go of all the resentment she harbored toward the people we had entrusted with our money, all the negative feelings of emotional abandonment carried over from her difficult childhood, and all her disappointments in others, she became free. She accepted her fate and never ever wavered, even in her final days.

Four days after learning the gravity of her illness and being admitted to the hospital, Carol accepted and embraced her destiny. The power and bliss that followed, from being able to detach, let go and totally surrender, was beyond words.

When Carol took her own leap of faith, she was giving it all to God. She accomplished this through a simple and powerful declaration:

"Here, God, take it all away from me. All this resentment I've been holding on to, all this disappointment I've kept bottled inside of me, all of this negative, polluted and poisonous energy that I've carried and that I've been dragging with me all my life—take it all away from me. Here it is. I'm done with all this crap. Take it all away!"

Carol meditated on that declaration until she felt truly free. Afterwards, she was in a state of peace, appreciation, gratitude, love, joy, happiness and complete bliss like I'd never seen in her before. How was it humanly possible for Carol to feel this way, considering the devastating news

Resentment robs you of joy, contentment and peace.

she'd just received? When there was no happy ending in sight? By the simple and powerful act of using faith and connecting with her higher power, she was able to rise and grow beyond herself!

The question we must ask ourselves is, "Why should I wait until I'm on the last chapter of my life to let go—to be liberated? What purpose could holding on to this hatred, this anger, this frustration, this resentment, this jealousy, this envy, this fear, this cruelty, this impatience, this worry, this anxiety, this mistrust, this sadness and this depression possibly serve? How could it serve me now and throughout my life to be free of it?"

Every time you become aware of feeling a negative emotion, ask your higher power to help you—give yourself permission to let go by asking and directing your higher power to take it all away from you. You'll be surprised how effective this can be. You may be sad, you may shed some tears, you may be hurt, or you may feel fragile, but when you repeat this simple act every time you feel any negative emotion, you will experience destructive feelings less and less over time. Simply stated, letting go will liberate you and accelerate your healing.

What enabled Carol to become liberated, free of all that resentment she had held for all those years, was her *total faith, total belief and total trust, which is the power of total conviction; that power enabled her to let go and totally detach.* She had to release it to someone greater than herself—to God, to her higher power—and she was able to do this through faith. And the result of this exercise was truly magical for her, during what was left of her short life.

What are your regrets? What are your fears? Who is it that you cannot forgive? What resentments are you holding on to? Holding on to this resentment robs you of joy, contentment and peace. It's a choice *you* make.

What good does holding on to resentment and negative sentiment serve you? Why wait to release yourself from this heavy burden that weighs on you each and every day?

WHEN YOU POSSESS NOTHING, YET HAVE EVERYTHING

Visiting poor villages in the Indian countryside, I saw firsthand how little the people who live there have. Some have nothing. Some sleep in or use nearby temples as their homes. They have no food, no possessions besides the clothes they wear. Yet they greeted me with sincere smiles when I approached them. When I looked in their eyes, I saw intense and resilient souls.

Despite their living conditions, they don't feel sorry for themselves; they can't. They can't permit themselves to sink into depression; this isn't an option they can contemplate. They don't know about Prozac and they certainly don't have access to it! Many of them wake each day with no idea where their next meal will come from. They have no safety net or support system. How could they possibly have time for self-pity?

What sustains them, what keeps them going—like the very heart of our soul that never misses a beat—is their spiritual connection to their higher power. This alone provides them with hope and fuels and sustains them each day. Their faith is all they have; it's all they know.

While visiting Thailand, I spent time exploring Bangkok and Chiang Mai. During my travels, and while visiting many Thai temples, I couldn't help but notice the internal beauty of the Thai people. They are all so friendly and happy, always smiling, and will try to do anything to be of help. Yet many of them are very poor and work very hard trying to make a living.

Thai taxi drivers are a good example of this. Bangkok has an abundance of taxi drivers, and if you've been there, you know the city's paralyzing traffic. Yet you can hire a taxi to drive you around for the equivalent of three dollars an hour. And they'll wait for you as you go from venue to venue. Just think, they have vehicles they need to maintain, and gas is as expensive there as it is in any other place in the world. Yet when we're stopped at a traffic light, here's a taxi driver buying a flower necklace from a young girl selling her goods on the street, and he places the necklace around his mirror as a spiritual symbol and performs a short prayer in honor of his higher power.

I remember noticing a man riding on a public bus. It was late in the day, right in the middle of "traffic hour" (which never stops in Bangkok, but simply heightens as five p.m. approaches). He seemed tired and was rubbing his eyes. But when the bus paused in front of a spiritual statue while waiting for traffic to clear, he bowed his head and recited a short prayer. It was simply a natural and unconscious act for him and for so many others I observed.

Practically every street corner in Thailand has a small area adorned by a statue of a spiritual figure, allowing people who use the streets many places of worship. Many use these street corner statues as sites where they pray before and after work, if only for a few minutes. Most don't have much. Most work very hard for very little in return. Yet they are among the happiest, most content, joyous and resilient people I've come across in all my travels.

The one thing they do have, and practice each day—it is constantly in their sight, mind and consciousness—is this spiritual connection that they take such pride in honoring in each passing moment during their difficult life journey. Bangkok alone has over four hundred temples and thousands of spiritual statues and monuments located throughout the city. These all serve as places of worship and constant reminders to remain consciously connected.

Poor people in India or Thailand don't have a lotto ticket on which to place their hope. They possess something much more powerful, much more sustainable—something that no one, no matter what, can take away from them.

Of all the attachments you could choose, this one will never cause you pain and suffering, because you'll never lose it or be threatened with its loss as long as you remain conscious of its existence. Never underestimate the power of faith and spiritual connection. Some I've observed have nothing—and yet they have everything!

YOU ARE MORE POWERFUL THAN YOU THINK YOU ARE

As I mentioned above, when it comes to seeing someone in pain, especially a child or someone close to me, my usual reaction is one of complete weakness. I start sweating and, if I don't sit down, I feel as though I am going to pass out. I remember way back when Carol had day surgery on something minor and elective. When I went to pick her up at the hospital, Carol had been sick from the anesthesia. As I stood in her room, I noticed she had gotten a little ill while lying down. The nurse went to help her, and I observed Carol wince from the pain of her surgery.

I started to feel weak and turned ghostly white. Carol looked at me and said to the nurse, "You better go take care of him, instead of me!" We all laughed, but this is how affected I was by this type of scenario.

Now imagine all that goes on both inside and outside the hospital with your loved one who is very sick from cancer. I'll spare you the details, but the point is that during this entire time with Carol, I had never been so strong in my life. Nothing bothered me, from changing dressings on an infected area of her body, to injecting blood-thinners to changing diapers, and so on.

I know that some of you would say, "So what?" But for me, comparing what I had experienced before to what I was able to do with Carol when she had cancer was remarkable, and the strength and resolve that I felt were greater than I could ever have imagined. It was bigger than me.

The final three weeks in the hospital were a roller coaster of emotions and difficulty. One minute you sense (and the doctors tell you) that the end could be anytime soon; the next

> *You possess all the ingredients, all the power, to overcome anything.*

moment you think it could be months away. No one knows when the transition will take place. Carol would have many good days and exceptional moments, and then things would go downhill, really fast.

Throughout this time, I remember feeling incredibly strong and in control and aware of everything that was happening. I was on top of everything, including all the pills and blood thinners that Carol required. I stayed on the nurses (in a polite but assertive way) to make sure that all was taking place as it should.

The nurses gave me a lot of leeway, as well; I was able to feed Carol, and sometimes, as long as we were basically on schedule, I'd let her sleep a little longer until she woke up on her own. Then I'd give her the medicine she needed. At the most difficult moments, I would feel a surge of strength. I felt that I possessed a new and perpetually regenerating energy.

I didn't sleep very well in the hospital, as you can imagine, and I often lacked any meaningful sleep for weeks, but it didn't seem to bother me one bit. I was simply generating the get-up-and-go I needed and never felt that I lacked energy. I never felt tired or worn out.

During our last days and moments together, after Carol's passing, and even while delivering her eulogy at her funeral, I still felt strong and empowered. I know this may sound odd, but I never felt more spiritually connected or closer to my higher power.

You may be facing a difficult situation right now that makes you feel weak or ill-prepared. You may believe that you aren't capable of handling whatever is required of you. I assure you that, with faith, you can overcome anything. You possess all the ingredients, all the power, to overcome anything. You simply need to recognize this power, harness it to the fullest and watch the magic take place. You are so much more powerful than you realize!

POWERFUL AND INCOMPREHENSIBLE

Envision how you can consciously connect with your higher power on a regular basis. Then use it to help you in every situation that life brings you and be grateful for that help, comfort, guidance and strength. Use it to help you detach from all the negative emotions that you hold on to so dearly and that are so damaging to you, and use it to live gratefully for all that you have. Be thankful and appreciate being alive— here and now!

What is your relationship with your higher power? What is your connection with your faith? How pure or corroded is that connection? Hear and feel the strength that faith and a higher power can bring you during your most difficult moments.

I remember asking Francine, "Were you, in that moment of the sexual assault, closer to God than at any other time in your life?"

Francine replied, "Oh, absolutely! It's what allowed me to stay calm and stop the attacker from hurting me.

"I met other women, one in particular that this same man had assaulted in a different hotel just a month before my assault. She had gone through eight reconstructive surgeries! This guy had disfigured her so badly... so was he able to create violence? No question about it! Did I sense that violent capability when I saw him at my door? No question that I knew this guy was a psychopath—and he was, and he proved it! He had absolutely no remorse whatsoever, and when the trial was over, we were in hearing distance of each other and here's what he said to me: 'My first inclination was to kill you, and I should have!' And I knew it... I knew that he was capable of killing me. He was the kind of guy that was up to no good, and he had that look where you actually can sense what someone may be capable of. That was not imaginary. I had confirmation of that 'sense' after finding out all the things he had been involved in, so having that kind of connection... absolutely.

"I felt totally guided, and that something so much bigger than me was protecting me. And if I was going to stay within that feeling and stay connected to that feeling... I needed to be really calm.

"There was a nurse at the women's hospital where they took me. She sat with me and said: 'You know, I see women all the time that come here that are disfigured and sometimes battered beyond recognition. Although I know we cannot undo what he has done to you emotionally, don't ever doubt your power! Your power is so strong that you were able to overcome his power, and that is nothing short of extraordinary!'

"But the most extraordinary thing in all of that was when it came time for me to leave the room for additional treatment. I wanted to say goodbye to her. And I said to another nurse, 'I want to say goodbye to the nurse that was here just a little while ago.' And she looked at me with this look on her face as if she wanted to say, 'What are you talking about, lady? I know that you've gone through trauma, but now you're losing it!' Instead she responded, 'What are you talking about?' And I said, 'The nurse... she was right next to me. You saw her! She was here!' And the nurse replied, 'There was never anyone else here. There was never anyone else in the room with us!' But I am telling you, this nurse was as real as you and I."

• • •

Francine's story is meant to be honored, not sensationalized. My hope in sharing her story is that you will receive it as one of inspiration and empowerment. Your situation and challenges are different and you will probably never have to face this type of assault and trauma. But you are facing difficulty and stressful situations, and Francine's story is here to demonstrate the potential and strength we all possess through faith, if we choose to connect with and harness it.

Having a strong connection and strong faith is one pillar that will help hold up this incredible fortress and resiliency you are building, no matter what comes your way.

In the world where we live today, it is easy to discount faith. It is easy to rely on our cognitive ability as we try to frame our experiences in a way we are able to understand. Faith has become an increasingly difficult concept for many to accept, and yet it is this Coping Principle that generates the power you will need to continue your quest in becoming Shatterproof.

Am I suggesting that you quit your job and become a devoted follower of a particular faith? No. Am I suggesting that you take time to figure out what it is that you believe and nurture that connection? Yes. Faith is as essential an ingredient in this journey as any other Coping Principle or activity, and may perhaps be even more important.

Faith is the cornerstone of our ability to take those things we are subject to and put them to work for us. It is our chance to bring meaning to the meaningless, to empower those experiences that we wish we did not have to endure.

For those of you who already embrace faith as a part of your lives, I hope you will see this as an affirmation of its importance in times of crisis. I hope that these lessons will show you how to better use your faith to quickly move from breakdown to breakthrough and become Shatterproof.

For those to whom faith is a foreign concept, I hope you will find some small seed of faith within that you can grow and nourish. And if nothing else, I hope you renew your faith in *yourself*—for that alone is a miracle.

• • •

Crisis is difficult. It can be painful; it can cause you to experience things you never hoped or even imagined you would have to endure. Your ability to exercise faith in these times may be the difference between your ultimate success and failure. Do not allow yourself to fall prey to the belief that you can do it without faith, or that you will address the nature of your faith later, when you need it, for those moments when you need faith are not the moments when you will be able to search it out. Build that muscle now. Make faith part of your daily journey so that when you do need it, you will find it waiting to help you get through your trial.

This is my hope for us all: that our faith will allow us to be the people we need to be. That it will bring us the same joy and peace that I have witnessed in so many people around the globe. That it will allow us to frame our crisis in such a way that we will recognize those things we can use to make our future better. If we can do that, we have won the prize. We have accomplished what many never do and we have taken a huge step on our journey to truly becoming Shatterproof.

Question your faith. Don't just accept it or dismiss it based on too few experiences, or through sheer laziness or ignorance. Nurture it. Challenge it. Challenge yourself. Consciously seek ways to expand and appreciate faith. And consciously seek the meaning that faith gives existence.

To experience faith is to nurture it. To nurture faith is to be in a state of awareness. Being aware and living in a state of gratitude and faith each and every day will cultivate a sense of peace and confidence within you that is unshakable and unsinkable. In this mindset, you're on the path to becoming Shatterproof!

1. How do you define faith and how do you practice it in your life?

2. Think about examples of faith in action in your life, times when you may have relied on faith or taken a "leap of faith." What were the outcomes?

3. How could you nurture your own faith in simple ways going forward?

Note: I created a free workbook for you, so that you can answer these and other questions and track your progress in one place. You'll also find helpful exercises. To download your free copy of *The Shatterproof Workbook*, go to shatterproofbook.com/resources.

Chapter 10

Beyond the Seven Coping Principles: Entering the Shatterproof Zone

Imagine walking through life with the ability to deflect stress, negative emotions and the general "noise" of the world, to bend when others break and to experience joy, love and happiness, even while enduring the most difficult circumstances. All of this is possible when you tap into the Shatterproof Zone.

The Shatterproof Zone is the flip side of the adrenalin-fused state we associate with peak performance. Stress can propel you into "the zone," enabling you to pull an all-nighter, win the race or lift a car off of a child. But can you turn it off? In today's society, more and more people are prisoners of their own minds, living in this stress-fueled zone, which dramatically alters their quality of life and puts them at risk for chronic disease.

The Shatterproof Zone is the eye of the hurricane, that place where you can remain calm, content and even peaceful, despite the chaos around you. When faced with stress or crisis, entering the Shatterproof Zone enables you to better able to manage fear of the unknown and loss of control; in this zone you are better equipped to find solutions and take action and, more importantly, you are able to stay present in the moment and fully experience the opportunity of the crisis.

When you are stuck in the stress zone, one unexpected crisis could break you. When you can tap into the Shatterproof Zone, nothing can break you.

When I first fully grasped the severity of Carol's condition, I was able to shift my mindset away from anxiety, fear and helplessness and activate the Shatterproof Zone. Drawing on a disciplined and focused mindset, techniques I had learned to help me de-stress and the Seven Coping Principles, which

This powerful tool, the mind,
determines your world.

by then had been completely ingrained in me, enabled me to be present for Carol and perform all of the tasks needed to support her. I wasn't a basket case; I was useful and calm and able to experience the journey purposefully. In this mindset, I was able to make good choices and recognize the blessings of the experience.

According to the *Psychology Today* article, "The Brain's Ability to Look Within: A Secret to Self-Mastery,"[6] humans have an inherent ability to calm ourselves down. I reference humans, but actually, this is an age-old ability we share with many animals. It involves shifting focus away from the external and toward the internal, and when we connect with this intrinsic ability, we are "tapping into bodily awareness that is free from social judgment or conceptual self-evaluation."

In the following pages, I'll explain how you can tap into this ability. Employing this and other techniques in a practice will give you easy and immediate access to the Shatterproof Zone. It's a bit like envisioning an impenetrable bubble around yourself that protects you and enables you to think clearly, so you can make proper decisions and take action.

This practice enables me to tune into calmness at will. Chaos might be around me, but not within me. I have full concentration and dictate where to direct my attention. I can completely tune out negativity and—similar to an athlete performing at peak during the last second of a match—achieve ultra-focus. In this state, in this Shatterproof Zone, the most impossible tasks suddenly seem doable and the most difficult crises suddenly seem manageable. It is remarkable.

YOU ARE ALREADY HALFWAY THERE...

If you've started practicing the Seven Coping Principles, you are already well on your way to developing the ability to enter the Shatterproof Zone. To recap:

> **First Coping Principle:** You learned how to instantly bring your mind into focus mode, becoming aware of your thoughts, words and actions. And you acknowledged that you are in a crisis or a difficult or stressful situation and are ready to face it.

> **Second Coping Principle:** You not only accepted the situation, you realized the value in embracing its potential opportunities. You are now creating an environment in which your mind is opening up, finding meaning in your stress, crisis or setback.

With this approach, you're taking steps to reduce or eliminate suffering from the experience.

Third Coping Principle: You forced yourself to ask, "Now what?" by navigating the worst-case scenario, regardless of your insecurities. You moved from fear to courage. You are facing the reality of your situation and shifting into problem-solving mode.

Fourth Coping Principle: You listed all of your worries and fears and faced your unresolved issues and an uncertain future. Then, you focused your mindset to choose the issues you could control, influence or change.

Fifth Coping Principle: You took action to create a different reality. You planned your approach, breaking it down into manageable tasks you control. Again, you looked for opportunities—the chance to start something new, to create a new vision for your life. You shifted your attention toward activities that serve you.

Sixth Coping Principle: You compiled a gratitude list that helps you stay rooted in the present. Focused in a state of gratitude and appreciation, your mind is free from a fractured and negative mindset.

Seventh Coping Principle: When you're feeling confident, when you feel empowered—when you *have faith* in your own power—you can confront and get through any difficult situation you may face. So how do you regain confidence when crisis has stripped it from you? How can you make it through unexpected stresses and events if it seems you've lost the ability to tap into your own power?

The answer is simple: faith in a power greater than yourself.

The Seven Coping Principles will serve you well—and they will serve you *best* when working in cooperation with a well-trained, focused and disciplined mind.

THE IMPORTANCE OF MANAGING THE MIND

Your mind is the most powerful and least measurable tool you possess. To effectively use this tool, you have to learn how to manage it. The mind is programmed by an accumulation of many things: upbringing; experiences and unresolved issues from the past; the prejudices, religions and other belief systems of family, social circle and community; and misconceptions and resentments.

This powerful tool, the mind, determines your world. Your mind affects your relationships, determines your successes and failures, creates happiness or misery—it even has an impact on your health. Your mind directly determines the quality of your life. There's no escaping your mind; you carry your mindset wherever you go. Do you see why it's so important that you learn how to manage this precious and powerful tool? Day in and day out, where you direct your attention creates your reality.

If you choose to focus on resentment, past hurt or disappointments, blaming others, anger, fear, doubt, worry, unfairness, getting even or proving you're right, then you are choosing to create a negative environment for yourself. You will probably find that your life is difficult, laborious, exhausting and mentally draining. You might hear yourself complain about being "unlucky" and respond to negativity with more negativity. And you'll inevitably have to deal with ailments and sickness.

Where you choose to direct your attention, where your mindset is focused and the emotions that accompany your thoughts will determine the type of journey you experience. Recall Elizabeth's story. Her mind was intentionally focused on creating a loving, peaceful and harmonious environment for herself and her son. She was successful in achieving her desired result because her mind and emotions were aligned and focused on creating what she envisioned. Equally important, Elizabeth didn't give in to anger at the world for her circumstances, or anger at her ex, her coworkers or her friends. She didn't look for revenge; she didn't want to engage in a fight that could not have a winner and didn't waste energy on trying to prove who was right or have the last word. None of those negative reactions would have served her; they would all have been contrary to what she was attempting to create for herself.

If you are able to follow Elizabeth's example and put this intention into practice, you will embark on a path that will serve you throughout your life. The problem is, many of us focus on negativity and align our emotions with that energy. It's not your fault; it's the way the mind is wired. The mind is programmed to protect us from threats most of us don't experience in our day-to-day lives and to worry about safety and react defensively. The mind also has a tendency to "wander" when the body is focused on other tasks. This is when spontaneous thoughts move in and out, without logic or direction. And when the mind wanders, it won't be long before it takes you down memory lane, back toward past issues, or toward an unknown and uncertain future.

In his *Science* Magazine article, "A Wandering Mind is an Unhappy Mind,"[7] Matt Killingsworth, PhD, Robert Wood Johnson Health and Society Scholar and founder of trackhappiness.org, shared the results of his study based on samples of people's ongoing thoughts, feelings and actions. Killingsworth found that "people are thinking about what is not happening almost as often as they are thinking about what is… and found that doing so typically makes them unhappy."

We are at our happiest when we are immersed in "present moment" experiences. And yet wandering mind is the brain's default mode—the mind wanders during roughly half of our waking hours—which means it is actually wired to take us out of the present moment, out of *happiness*.

PROTECTING YOUR MIND FROM EXHAUSTION

The mind may be the most powerful tool we possess, but we haven't yet learned how to harness its power. Instead, we are programmed to wander toward negative thoughts, which cause a stressful mindset. Further, we have developed habits that hinder our ability to gain a disciplined mindset.

In life today, we all have to attend to too many demands, deadlines, duties and responsibilities. The advent and advancement of technologies, smart devices and social pressures and expectations require us to face a barrage of distractions as we are pulled in various directions, day in and day out.

All of this will likely lead you to feel various degrees of stress, which is often accumulative. You may leave work feeling exhausted and mentally drained. You may have trouble sleeping. You may feel anxious or tired; you may get sick easily. Over time, it may even seem as though stress is just a way of life, the norm, something that can't be avoided.

While the noise and demands of life may be inevitable— unless you move off the grid and live like a hermit!—the way you choose to cope with your work and life demands *is* within your power to control. It is imperative for your health and well-being that you learn how to gain that control, if you want to survive and strive in today's stress-induced environment.

Before learning how to gain that control, let's examine some of the habits we've adopted that inhibit a controlled and disciplined mind.

THE MULTITASKING MYTH

Over the years, most of us have developed a skill that is now "required" for most jobs: multitasking. The notion was, if we could multitask, we could increase productivity. In fact, multitasking achieves the exact opposite. The *Wall Street Journal* article, "The Inner Workings of the Executive Brain,"[8] explains that, contrary to popular belief, your conscious mind can only perform one thing (one calculation) at a time. That is the way the brain is wired. Although the mind is very quick, and gives the appearance of doing many things at once, it can only do one.

Multitasking takes you out of the present by diverting your attention. Over time, a fractured mindset drains your energy. You become less efficient and less productive. You can't achieve "peak performance" in this state. A fractured mindset equals fractured results.

Multitasking gives you a false sense of productivity and efficiency. Instead, it can cause real damage. Research concludes that multitasking can destroy the brain over time. There are many studies available that support this theory. The journal *Intelligence* published one 2010 study,

> *A fractured mindset equals fractured results.*

"Intelligence, Working Memory and Multitasking,"[9] which concluded that, while juggling multiple tasks, you use a lot of working memory and "executive control"—the ability to direct and focus your attention. Working memory involves attention, concentration, mental control and reasoning. We only have so much working memory at our disposal. By taxing your working memory and your ability to focus, multitasking actually blocks your ability to engage new ideas, which is necessary when attempting to find solutions to problems, and thus diminishes your productivity and potential.[10, 11]

When you're multitasking, you divide your attention in two or more areas. As an example, think about having to and respond to text messages, instant messaging or a Facebook message while working on a document, executive summary or spreadsheet. Each disruption causes your short-term memory to fade. According to the *Business Journal* article, "Too Many Interruptions at Work?"[12], it can take close to twenty-three minutes to get back on task. Straining your working memory to restart and switching your attention to the task at hand requires effort. Every distraction adds stress and causes your work performance to suffer, and this will eventually take an emotional toll on you.

Today's working environment is loaded with necessary and unnecessary disruptions from colleagues, managers and executives pinging employees for updates frequently during the day. We are often required to attend unproductive meetings and handle hundreds of emails daily. All these inefficiencies, disruptions and time-wasters add up and require a degree of working memory to navigate. No wonder you leave work feeling exhausted and burned out!

WEIGHED DOWN WITH UNFINISHED TASKS

According to Roy F. Baumeister and John Tierney, the authors of the bestselling book *Willpower: Rediscovering the Greatest Human Strength*,[13] "At any one time, a person typically has at least 150 different tasks to be done, and fresh items never stop appearing on our screens." Wow! A to-do list of more than 150 items of uncompleted tasks and goals at any one time! That's a heavy burden to carry, and for you to worry about when your mind wanders. Aren't you exhausted just thinking about it? When your mind drifts to all these open and unfinished projects throughout the day, your attention deviates from the task at hand, from the one thing you should be doing, which prevents you from efficiently moving through that monster to-do list.

THE DEADLINE MYTH

Just as multitasking is counterproductive, so are deadlines. The prevailing wisdom is that a deadline will help you focus on getting the job done.[14] In reality, tight deadlines increase urgency and stress levels. The more stressful the deadline, the less open you are to other ways of approaching the problem; the deadline then becomes counterproductive. Just when you need people to be more creative in their problem-solving, the deadline limits thinking and can lead to poor decision-making. In fact, *The Mayo Clinic Guide to Stress-Free Living*[15] states that "more than two thirds of business decisions are wrong and unproductive and require future action to correct their efforts."

Deadlines, multitasking, unfinished tasks, mind-wandering and the use of smart devices are not going to go away. They are part of our everyday lives. But there is a penalty to be paid in becoming easily distracted. An undisciplined mindset not only affects you physically and mentally, but also affects your relationship connections, your creative process and overall productivity and output.

THE COST IMPACT

Putting an estimated cost figure on that penalty is no easy task, but common sense tells us that it's got to be high. Basex, Inc., an IT research company, did a study on the knowledge worker (office workers and professionals), and in terms of loss, productivity and innovation, the estimated cost of information overload is $588 billion a year in the United States alone.[16] Now that's a BIG number, and if you're employed as a knowledge worker, you are part of that number.

THE PRESENT MOMENT CATALYST

What's the answer? According to the *Psychology Today* article, "The Brain's Ability to Look Within: A Secret to Self-Mastery,"[17] various research indicates that our greatest moments of happiness are times we spend fully involved and engaged in a situation, whether it is a physical activity, a sensory experience or an experience of intimacy with another person. If we permit ourselves to become easily distracted, we are depriving ourselves of some of the greatest sources of happiness. In *A Wandering Mind is an Unhappy Mind,* Killingsworth and Gilbert concluded that when we're engaged fully in "present-moment awareness" we are at our happiest, stating, "Being present influenced happiness up to four times more."[18] So how can we put ourselves in a position to be present more frequently?

Throughout this book, you've heard me say that the body believes what the mind thinks. If you want to achieve and maintain a healthy body and a healthy mind, it is imperative that you actively choose what to direct your mind to think and where to direct your mind to focus. The answer lies in bringing awareness to your "focus" mindset. *The Mayo Clinic's Guide to Stress-Free Living* informs us that "when you are awake, your whole brain works in two modes—focused or default."[19]

Imagine you are walking through an airport, killing time while waiting for your plane, when you run into an old friend you haven't seen in years. Your mind is totally focused on reconnecting with your friend, and in this state, time just flies by. The same thing happens when I play a game of hockey. When I'm on the ice, I'm totally immersed in the experience of the game; my mind is totally focused on the present moment. The same focus can be achieved when reading a good book, or playing an action-packed video game or concentrating on a physical task you have to complete.

The Mayo Clinic's Guide to Stress-Free Living states, "focused thinking creatively solves a problem, savors an experience or contemplates a higher principle."[20] In this state, your mind is actively focused and you're fully immersed in the experience. When you choose, direct and are aware of your thoughts, your focused mode dominates, leading you to a healthier and a more positive experience. And when you stop focusing and lose awareness, your mind automatically goes back to default mode: wandering.

Your mind naturally switches from focused to wandering at a moment's notice. But rather than let this happen passively, why not learn how to activate your focus mindset so you can experience the peace and happiness provided by the present moment more frequently? By moving the needle ever so slightly from wandering to active focus, you create a more enjoyable journey. As Elizabeth created her vision for herself and her son, you can create your own bright, joyful future. You can do this by training your mind and shifting your thinking.

Imagine gaining control of your spontaneous thoughts while enjoying a more pleasant and positive dialogue internally. Imagine achieving a more purposeful and productive life, filled with vitality, happiness and contentment. Imagine noticing and embracing the little things that make life worth living, and being filled with appreciation and a sense of abundance. Imagine being actively present more frequently. What impact would that have on your relationships? Your health? Your peace of mind? Your aspirations? Your career and work experiences?

The more you experience the present, the more fun you'll have. With your mind firmly rooted in the present moment, you can experience it fully; you can truly get the most out of life. That *is* what that expression means. It's not about attaining a goal; it's about being fully present so you can experience each moment to the fullest. String a few moments, a hundred moments, a thousand, a million fully present moments together and you experience joy beyond imagining.

THE SHATTERPROOF PRACTICES: TRAINING THE MIND

To establish a focused and disciplined mindset so that you can enter the Shatterproof Zone at a moment's notice, you need to train your mind. This is no different than learning to play a new sport such as tennis, golf or skating. You need to develop new skills to be able to enjoy and participate in the game. And that happens with training and regular practice before you become proficient and get to a point where it becomes natural for you. With awareness and practice, you'll be able to shift your thinking by drawing your attention to areas that will serve you positively.

The *Globe and Mail* article, "Are You Struggling to Cope with the Stress of Work and Life?" cites a recent study by Howatt HR Consulting that found that coping skills are a lead indicator for predicting employee productivity, engagement and health. The study found that people with strong coping skills are more productive, more engaged in their work, and healthier.[21] Once you learn and develop skills to cope with the stress of life and work, you can then tackle and change your eating habits, exercise habits, smoking, drinking and drug habits and reduce your reliance on medication. Trying to fix these habits without first learning to develop coping skills will often result in failure or fleeting success that is simply unsustainable.

The Seven Coping Principles are designed to not only give you skills to handle most crises and stressful situations, but also to help you experience a joyful life and create a better future for yourself. The Coping Principles are valuable long after you have weathered whatever storms you've experienced. Use them; they will benefit you greatly.

You will also have to train your mind in order to accelerate your growth. When you practice the Seven Coping Principles and train your mind to be more focused and disciplined, you will be able to effortlessly tap into the Shatterproof Zone. And the fun part is, while learning to develop a focused and disciplined mindset, you'll experience relaxation and calm on a regular basis, allowing your body and mind to decompress and heal while releasing stress.

My mind-training came through learning and practicing a series of exercises and techniques that were geared toward reducing stress, along with following instructions in guided meditation and mindfulness. After more than twenty-five years learning and practicing with the help of a master teacher—some of these teachings date back five thousand years—I have become aware that the body (with the help of the mind) has the ability to self-regulate and heal if only we allow it, if only we give it a chance. And I've discovered that there are thousands of ways to meditate.

I remember the first time Carol and I attended our first class on learning to de-stress and relax. We had to drive at least thirty minutes to get there, and the class was held on Friday nights from seven to nine p.m.! Now, when you're through with your work week and it's Friday night, getting in a car to drive for thirty minutes or more to attend a relaxation and de-stressing class isn't the most appealing idea. Still, we dragged each other out there to try it.

We arrived at that first class tired and hungry, but within five minutes we realized we had made the right decision. We could feel a shift almost immediately. After two hours of class, I walked out feeling more energized than I had felt all week; I was in a state of relaxation and contentment, feeling at peace. (To this day, I still can't figure out why we felt no hunger pangs during that class.) I was hooked. Whatever that was, I wanted more of it. I needed more of it!

What was profoundly amazing to me was that the feeling of contentment remained throughout the weekend, but its quality shifted. I started to notice little things that I had not noticed before. I was far more aware of my surroundings and the beauty that existed there. It was as if I had put on a new set of glasses and was able to see some things for the first time. The external noise we were exposed to every day quietened, the chaos tempered. I knew they existed, but they didn't affect me, as if I had pushed the "mute" button on the stressful aspects of the world around me.

I wondered, *Could this feeling be sustained?* That's when I made a decision and a commitment to learn more about these practices and techniques so I could incorporate them into my everyday life. The possibility of having control of a peaceful and focused state despite the stress and distractions I was exposed to every day excited me.

With the help of my master teacher and a specialized team, I've synthesized all the experiences and teachings I've received over the last twenty-five years, taking morsels of five thousand year-old ancient Eastern teachings from China, Thailand and India, combining these with Western knowledge and science and embedded it all into a practical program geared for today's stressful and busy lifestyle. It's a series of exercises and techniques designed to train the mind (and body) under the umbrella "Shatterproof Practices."

The Shatterproof Practices are bite-sized chunks— practical techniques that will help you take baby steps toward bringing your mind into focus. With training and awareness, these practices will anchor you. With practice, you'll easily move from wandering mind to shifting and directing your thoughts, drawing your attention to more productive and purposeful areas that will serve you better. In time, your focused mindset will dominate on a more conscious level.

For example, one of the Shatterproof Practices is a "Time Out Moment," a five-minute exercise designed to force you to take a mental break during your busy workday. This guided process will help you de-stress and recharge your batteries while enhancing your ability to solve problems with mental clarity. You'll gain a sense of control, increase your productivity, feel more satisfied and find more enjoyment in your task at hand and your day-to-day activities.

The Shatterproof Practices are also designed to help you balance the variety of negative emotions that you may often experience throughout a nutty and stressful day. Imagine learning to defuse the tension that accompanies negative emotions such as anger, fear, impatience, anxiety and sadness. Each one of these emotions has a profound effect on your organs, such as your liver, kidneys, heart, stomach and lungs. Each organ correlates with a negative emotion, and once you know that, you can counter an emotion's impact before it harms you and affects your health.

As part of the exercises and meditation practices, you will be taught to create your very own sanctuary, a place you'll be able to mentally connect with at a moment's notice. The creation of your sanctuary plays an essential role in anchoring you when things get out of hand and when you want to tap into your Shatterproof Zone.

You'll also be guided in letting go from any person or thing you may find difficult to detach from.

To help you develop your skill in training your undisciplined mindset, every meditation exercise and technique is guided. If you simply try meditating to quiet the mind, at first, it won't work. Your undisciplined mind will simply start wandering, causing you frustration. The Shatterproof Practices allow you to go at your own pace as you gain a more focused mindset. This will enhance your ability to become more present throughout your day. It will help you improve your planning and decision-making skills, as well as heighten your empathy and love factor. You will feel less stress, while improving your level of patience. Your focus and memory will improve, and you'll find it easier to resist distractions. You'll gain the ability to sustain attention and concentration and to exert mental control while performing your daily tasks and responsibilities. You will build inner strength to tackle with confidence and clarity any challenges or events that could turn your world upside down. You will improve your ability to accomplish your goals on a regular basis.

The Shatterproof Practices introduce you to a number of techniques, and, after being exposed to them, you'll gravitate to the ones that you find most comfortable, natural, and easy to work with.

Other highlights included in the Shatterproof Practices are:

- Goal-setting techniques for achievement in every area of your life.
- Communication techniques that facilitate and enhance your connection with others.
- Simple techniques to eliminate procrastination.
- Decision-making techniques.
- Creativity-enhancing techniques and exercises.
- Motivation-enhancing techniques.
- Techniques for improvement of your self-image and overall confidence.
- Techniques for improving your self-esteem.
- Mind exercises designed to overcome your fears, such as fear of speaking in public.
- Various techniques and exercises designed to help you manage and deal with all the negative emotions present in your life.

Some of you may be asking why the Shatterproof Practices techniques and exercises are not included in this book. The answer is simple: because it wouldn't serve you. It's a bit like teaching you how to swim. No book can teach you how to swim. You need to be guided in the water to learn how to swim. You need to be guided with instructions using audio or video, or in person, to get the most out of the Shatterproof Practices. Simply reading about them won't do you much good. I'm only interested in offering you a program that can serve you and is sustainable for you. And you'll get to try it for free. (Go to shatterproof.me for your free demo.)

This Shatterproof process can be useful and help you in your everyday life. It makes no difference what activity you are

*Every time you worry, you
automatically generate stress.*

performing; whether it's a routine task or a highly demanding, pressure-packed responsibility, letting your mind drift uncontrolled will often lead you to feel worried and anxious, and soon enough doubt will start creeping in to erode your confidence. That worried mindset now generates stress. In fact, every time you worry, you automatically generate stress.

Healing is part of our existence. Our bodies were made to activate the healing process. Remember, the body believes what the mind thinks. Therefore, the mind plays a fundamental role in the healing process, including the healing of our emotions.

In a short time, with guidance and practice, your default mode will become more focused as opposed to wandering-mind. You'll develop and enjoy a disciplined mindset that you'll be able to connect with at a moment's notice.

Follow the Shatterproof Practices, or follow *The Mayo Clinic's Guide to Stress-Free Living,* or follow some other program—just don't let your mind go without guidance or direction. You have a choice to make. Do nothing, and continue experiencing a life filled with stress, anxiety, fear, worry, anger, impatience, sadness or depression. Or do something, and observe the change and experience vitality, joy, contentment, excitement, rejuvenation, calm and confidence and see the improvement in your relationships, your productivity and your positive impact on the world. It's a simple shift in thinking, and it all starts with awareness... which brings us back to the First Coping Principle!

Now that you see the advantage of a focused and disciplined mind, you can also see that you have been working on this all along. Each of the Seven Coping Principles helps train your

> *The mind plays a fundamental role in the healing process.*

mind and bring you back to the present moment. Incorporating the Seven Coping Principles and the Shatterproof Practices into your everyday life is the key to becoming Shatterproof.

IN CLOSING

As I said in the introduction, it's taken me more than five years to write *Shatterproof.* Before my research began, I knew the Seven Coping Principles worked—I had applied them over the last twenty years during my most difficult and stressful situations. I didn't have scientific proof, and wasn't seeking it because of the way I felt and what the Coping Principles did for me. The strength, power, courage and confidence they allowed me to harness throughout my most difficult periods was simply remarkable, and all the proof I needed.

Eventually, I found the proof—in countless articles and in *The Mayo Clinic's Guide to Stress-Free Living* and other books. And I encourage you to do your own research. Begin that research the way I did—by practicing what you've learned. Then seek further growth, whether with my guidance and the Shatterproof Practices, or by using another tool that will help you develop a focused and disciplined mind. Now that you are well on your way to becoming Shatterproof, it's time for you to begin your own journey toward wellness, fulfillment and unadulterated joy.

SHATTERPROOF FRAMEWORK

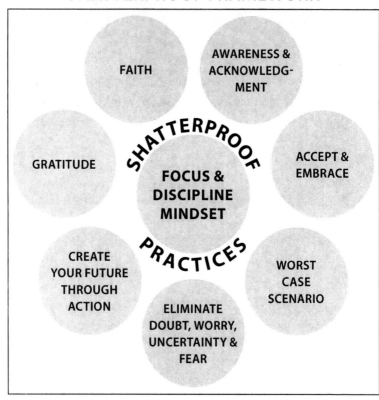

The Shatterproof Framework in Brief

The Shatterproof Framework is a combination of the Seven Coping Principles with the Shatterproof Practices. The Seven Coping Principles will serve you best when working in cooperation with a well-trained, focused and disciplined mind. Under the umbrella Shatterproof Practices, using a series of exercises and techniques, you'll learn to take baby steps towards bringing your mind into focus.

SEVEN COPING PRINCIPLES RECAP

1. **Awareness and Acknowledgment:** You learned how to instantly bring your mind into focus, and became aware of your thoughts, words and actions. You acknowledged that you are in a crisis or a difficult or stressful situation and that you are ready to face it.

2. **Accept and Embrace:** You not only accepted your current situation, you realized the value in embracing its potential opportunities. You are now

creating an environment in which your mind is opening up, and finding meaning in your stress, crisis or setback. With this approach, you're taking steps to reduce or eliminate suffering from the experience.

3. **Worst Case Scenario:** You forced yourself to ask, "Now what?" by navigating the worst-case scenario, regardless of your insecurities. You moved from fear to courage. You are facing the reality of your situation and shifting into problem-solving mode.

4. **Eliminate Doubt, Worry, Uncertainty and Fear:** You listed all of your worries and fears and faced your unresolved issues and an uncertain future. Then, you focused your mindset to choose the issues you could control, influence or change.

5. **Create Your Future Through Action:** You took action to create a different reality. You planned your approach, and broke it down into manageable tasks you control. Again, you looked for opportunities: the chance to start something new, to create a new vision for your life. You shifted your attention toward activities that serve you.

6. **Gratitude:** You compiled a gratitude list that helps you stay rooted in the present. Focused in a state of gratitude and appreciation, your mind is free from a fractured and negative mindset.

7. **Faith:** When you're feeling confident, when you feel empowered—when you have faith in your own power—you can confront and get through any difficult situation you may face. So how do you regain confidence when crisis has stripped it from you? How can you make it through unexpected stresses and events if it seems you've lost the ability to tap into your own power? The answer is simple: faith in a power greater than yourself.

How you choose to cope with your work and life demands is within your power to control, and your health and well-being depend on your choices. The Shatterproof Framework will help you gain the control you need to survive and thrive in any situation.

ENDNOTES

[1] Jeanne Segal, Melinda Smith, Robert Segal, and Lawrence Robinson, "Stress Symptoms Causes and Effects," accessed November 16, 2011, http://www.HelpGuide.org/articles/stress/stresssymptoms-causes-and-effects.htm.

[2] WebMD.com. "The Effects of Stress on Your Body," accessed November 16, 2011. http://www.webmd.com/balance/stressmanagement/effects-of-stress-on-your-body.

[3] Sue Shellenger, "When Stress is Good for You," *Wall Street Journal,* accessed January 24, 2012, http://www.wsj.com/articles/SB10001424052970204301404577171192704005250

[4] Michael Murray, "Two New Studies Show the Power of Gratitude and Kindness," accessed May 18, 2012, http://doctormurray.com/twonew-studies-show-the-power-of-gratitude-and-kindness/.

[5] Jennifer Goodwin, "After $75,000, Money Can't Buy Day-to-Day Happiness," *HealthDay Reporter,* accessed September 6, 2010, https://consumer.healthday.com/public-health-information-30/demographics-news-173/after-75-000-money-can-t-buy-day-to-day-happiness-642850.html

[6] Emma M. Seppala, "The Brain's Ability to Look Within: A Secret to Self-Mastery," *Psychology Today,* December 10, 2012, accessed January 10, 2013, https://www.psychologytoday.com/ blog/feeling-it/201212/the-brains-ability-look-within-secretself-mastery.

[7] Matthew A. Killingsworth, and Daniel T Gilbert, "A Wandering Mind is an Unhappy Mind," www.sciencemag.org, accessed December 14, 2014, http://science.sciencemag.org/content/330/6006/932.full?sid=3d27f229-6e05-4828-b560-1516e79f2a4d

[8] Andrew Blackman, "The Inner Workings of the Executive Brain," *Wall Street Journal,* accessed April 27, 2014, http://www.wsj.com/articles/the-inner-workings-of-the-executive-brain-1398388537

9. Roberto Colom, Agustin Martinez-Molina, Pei Chun Shih, and José Santacreu, "Intelligence, Working Memory and Multitasking Performance," accessed January 23, 2014, http://www.sciencedirect.com/science/article/pii/S0160289610001078

10. Sue Shellenbarger, "New Studies Show Pitfalls of Doing Too Much at Once," *Wall Street Journal,* accessed December 12, 2012, http://online.wsj.com/article/SB1046286576946413103.html

11. Sue Shellenbarger, "Why Multitasking Blocks Your Best Ideas," *Wall Street Journal,* accessed April 4, 2013, http://blogs.wsj.com/juggle/2013/04/04/why-multitasking-blocks-your-best-ideas/

12 Jennifer Robison, "Too Many Interruptions at Work?" *Business Journal* (2006), accessed October 31, 2013, http://www.gallup.com/businessjournal/23146/too-many-interruptions-work.aspx

13 Roy F. Baumeister and John Tierney, *Willpower: Rediscovering the Greatest Human Strength* (New York: Penguin, 2011), page 62.

14 Andrew Blackman, "The Inner Workings of the Executive Brain," *Wall Street Journal,* accessed April 27, 2014, http://www.wsj.com/articles/the-inner-workings-of-the-executive-brain-1398388537

15 Amit Sood, *The Mayo Clinic Guide to StressFree Living* (Massachusetts: De Cap Press, 2013), page 31.

16 Jonathan B. Spira and Joshua B. Feintuch, "The Cost of Not Paying Attention: How interruptions Impact Knowledge Worker Productivity", accessed May 7, 2012, http://iorgforum.org/wp-content/uploads/2011/06/CostOfNotPayingAttention.BasexReport.pdf

17 Emma M. Seppala, "The Brain's Ability to Look Within: A Secret to Self-Mastery," *Psychology Today* (2012): accessed January 10, 2013https://www.psychologytoday.com/ blog/feeling-it/201212/the-brains-ability-look-within-secretself-mastery.

[18] Matthew A. Killingsworth, and Daniel T Gilbert, "A Wandering Mind is an Unhappy Mind," www.sciencemag.org, accessed December 14, 2014, http://science.sciencemag.org/content/330/6006/932.full?sid=3d27f229-6e05-4828-b560-1516e79f2a4d

[19] Amit Sood, *The Mayo Clinic Guide to StressFree Living* (Massachusetts: De Cap Press, 2013,) page 3.

[20] Ibid, page 6.

[21] Bill Howatt, "Are You Struggling to Cope with the Stress of Work and Life?" May 5, 2014, accessed February 2014, http://www.theglobeandmail.com/report-on-business/careers/career-advice/life-at-work/areyou-struggling-to-cope-with-the-stress-of-work-and-life/article18469369.

BIBLIOGRAPHY

Baumeister, Roy F., and John Tierney. *Willpower: Rediscovering the Greatest Human Strength*. (New York: Penguin, 2011).

Blackman, Andrew. "The Inner Workings of the Executive Brain." *Wall Street Journal,* April 27, 2014.

Colom, Roberto, Agustin Martinez-Molina, Pei Chun Shih, and José Santacreu. "Intelligence, Working Memory and Multitasking Performance." *Intelligence* 38 (2010): 543- 551.

Goodwin, Jennifer. "After $75,000, Money Can't Buy Day-to-Day Happiness." *HealthDay Reporter,* September 6, 2010.

Howatt, Bill. "Are You Struggling to Cope with the Stress of Work and Life?" *The Globe and Mail,* May 5, 2014. Accessed February 2014. http://www.theglobeandmail.com/ report-on-business/careers/career-advice/life-at-work/are-you-struggling-to-cope-with-the-stress-of-work-and-life/ article18469369/.

Killingsworth, Matthew A., and Daniel T. Gilber., "A Wandering Mind is an Unhappy Mind." *Science,* November 12, 2010, 932.

Murray, Michael. "Two New Studies Show the Power of Gratitude and Kindness." Accessed May 18, 2012. http://doctormurray. com/two-new-studies-show-the-power-of-gratitude-and-kindness/.

Robison, Jennifer. "Too Many Interruptions at Work?" *Business Journal* (2006): Accessed October 31, 2013.

Segal, Jeanne, Melinda Smith, Robert Segal, and Lawrence Robinson. "Stress Symptoms Causes and Effects." Accessed November 16, 2011. http://www.HelpGuide.org/articles/stress/ stress-symptoms-causes-and-effects.htm.

Seppala, Emma M. "The Brain's Ability to Look Within: A Secret to Self-Mastery." *Psychology Today* (December 10, 2012). Accessed January 10, 2013. https://www.psychologytoday.

com/blog/feeling-it/201212/the-brains-ability-look-within-secretself-mastery.

Shellenbarger, Sue. "New Studies Show Pitfalls of Doing Too Much at Once." *Wall Street Journal,* February 27, 2003.

Shellenbarger, Sue. "When Stress is Good for You." *Wall Street Journal,* January 24, 2012.

Shellenbarger, Sue. "Why Multitasking Blocks Your Best Ideas." *Wall Street Journal,* April 4, 2013.

Sood, Amit. *The Mayo Clinic Guide to Stress-Free Living.* (Massachusetts: De Cap Press, 2013).

Spira, Jonathan B., and Joshua B. Feintuch. *The Cost of Not Paying Attention: How Interruptions Impact Knowledge Worker Productivity.* (New York: Basex, Inc., 2005).

WebMD.com. "The Effects of Stress on Your Body." Accessed November 16, 2011. http://www.webmd.com/balance/stress-management/effects-of-stress-on-your-body.

CPSIA information can be obtained
at www.ICGtesting.com
Printed in the USA
LVOW11s1531060418
572529LV00007B/152/P